C000143307

The
Shropshire
Village Book

THE VILLAGES OF BRITAIN SERIES
Other counties in this series include

The Shropshire Village Book

Compiled by the Shropshire
Federation of Women's Institutes
from notes and illustrations sent
by Institutes in the County

Published jointly by
Countryside Books, Newbury
and the S.F.W.I., Shrewsbury

First published 1988
© Shropshire Federation of Women's Institutes 1988

Countryside Books
3 Catherine Road
Newbury, Berkshire

ISBN 1 85306 030 5

Cover photograph of Little Stretton
taken by Margaret Palgrave

Produced through MRM Associates, Reading
Typeset by Acorn Bookwork, Salisbury
Printed in England by J. W. Arrowsmith Ltd., Bristol

Foreword

'There, somewhere, nor-nor-east from me
Was Shropshire where I longed to be
Ercall and Mynd
Severn, Wrekin, you and me'
John Masefield

The county of Shropshire is justly proud to be called one of the most attractive counties in England. Bounded by no fewer than eight counties, four of them Welsh, its richly varied countryside is steeped in history.

The river Severn curvingly divides the county into two equal parts. To the north east are the rolling acres of fertile agricultural land, while to the south west lies the hill country – Clee, Wenlock Edge, Caradoc, Long Mynd and Stiperstones. The Wrekin, which is known as the 'father' of English mountains, rises above the plain – a nostalgic symbol for all exiled Salopians and the inspiration for the traditional toast 'All friends round the Wrekin'.

Charting the history of this fascinating county, blessed with so many lovely villages, has been a most enjoyable experience which has required the goodwill and cooperation of all members of The Shropshire Federation of Women's Institutes.

We know that the contributors have derived great satisfaction from their task. We hope all who read the result will share our pleasure in this indispensable guide to our county and that it will give them a taste of the real Shropshire.

Betty Carlyle
Project Co-ordinator

Acknowledgements

The Shropshire Federation of Women's Institutes wish to thank all Institutes whose members worked very hard to research and provide information and drawings for their villages.

A special thank you to Betty Carlyle, who co-ordinated the project, together with Jean Bebb, Wendy Doyle, Anne Pipkin and Freda Riley.

SHROPSHIRE

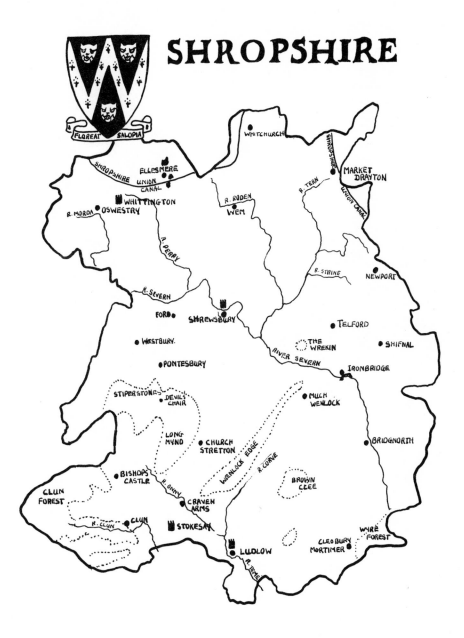

FLOREAT SALOPIA

WHITCHURCH

SHROPSHIRE UNION CANAL

ELLESMERE

MARKET DRAYTON

R. TERN

UNION CANAL

WHITTINGTON

R. RODEN

WEM

R. MORDA   OSWESTRY

R. PERRY

R. STRINE

NEWPORT

R. SEVERN

FORD   SHREWSBURY

TELFORD

WESTBURY.

THE WREKIN

SHIFNAL

RIVER SEVERN

PONTESBURY

IRONBRIDGE

STIPERSTONES

DEVIL'S CHAIR

MUCH WENLOCK

LONG MYND

CHURCH STRETTON

WENLOCK EDGE

R. CORVE

BRIDGNORTH

BISHOPS CASTLE

R. ONNY

BROWN CLEE

CLUN FOREST

CRAVEN ARMS

R. CLUN   CLUN

STOKESAY

WYRE FOREST

CLEOBURY MORTIMER

LUDLOW

R. TEME

LILLESHALL ABBEY

Acton Burnell 🌿

Acton Burnell is a picturesque village some 8 miles south east of Shrewsbury with a population of about 155 inhabitants.

The name Acton Burnell seems to have come from Ac-tune, meaning Oak-town. The Burnell part of the name commemorates Robert Burnell, who was Bishop of Bath and Wells at the end of the 13th century. He obtained a licence to build himself a partly-fortified manor house in Acton Burnell. Its ruins, now incorrectly called a castle, still stand in near proximity to the church.

In the parkland nearby, and visible from the church and the castle, are the end walls of a central hall of an earlier structure. It must have been a very large hall – the space between the two gables is about 157 feet × 40 feet – and it is said that here in 1283 Edward I called the first Parliament to which the Commons were summoned. Local people to this day refer to the two gable ends as those of Parliament Barn.

The church of St Mary has been described as one of the most complete 13th century churches in Britain. The monuments include one with alabaster effigies to Sir Richard Lee (1591) and Sir Humphrey Lee (1632), forebears of Robert E. Lee of American Civil War fame.

The large house (Acton Burnell Hall) near the church and the castle was the home of the Smythe family for many decades. At the outbreak of the Second World War in 1939 the Sisters of the Order of Sion established their Convent there and formed a girls school which continued until about 1970 when the nuns vacated the Hall. It then remained empty for several years before being opened as Concord College, a further education college catering mainly for overseas students.

The village shop was for many years kept by the Perks family but is now run, together with the post office, in conjunction with the college. Of course since the advent of supermarkets, people are not so dependent on shopping in villages but it would be sad to see the village shops disappear.

Acton Round 🌿

Although scarcely large enough to be called a village, the small hamlet of Acton Round sits on a hillside about 6 miles from Bridgnorth. Reached by a narrow lane leaving the A458 at Muckley Cross, it is little more than a handful of houses with a delightful old church and an attractive manor house, slumbering quietly away from the mainstream of life.

There has been a settlement on the site for a thousand years or more. It is recorded in the Domesday Book as Achetune which is generally accepted as meaning Oak-town and perhaps one of the oaks which gave it that name is the very ancient tree which can be discovered by walking about ¾ mile along the track which passes the church. This venerable oak has a girth of 29 feet and though short in stature and split, it is one of the oldest and largest unsupported oaks in the county, and has obviously been there for many centuries.

Acton Round Hall, built of mellow brick in 1714, was meant to serve the Acton family of Aldenham Park, about two miles away, as a Dower House, although it was very little used for this purpose. It has suffered little restoration and has remained virtually unchanged in appearance. However, visitors to Acton Round are somewhat surprised to find modern follies in a field across from the Hall, such as a pagoda, erected just a few years ago. Inside the Hall, which is open on certain afternoons, there is a collection of animal trophies – where else will you find an ape swinging from the chandelier and a giraffe's neck and head on the staircase wall?

The present church, hidden away amongst trees behind the Hall, is built of stone, topped with a small timber-framed belfry and dates from the 16th century. Two hundred years later a small chapel was added on the north side and contains monuments relating to the Acton family. Although very simple, the church is charming, with an air of quiet serenity and is well worth seeking out.

Acton Scott 🌿

Acton Scott was put on the map in 1975 when the Working Farm Museum opened to demonstrate farming and rural life in late 19th century South Shropshire. Many traditional country crafts are demonstrated from beekeeping to woodturning. The Farm Museum was originally the Home Farm of the Acton Scott estate belonging to the Acton family, who have owned land in Acton Scott since the 13th century. The Home Farm was farmed on behalf of the Lord Of The Manor to provide for the needs of the Hall and to enable him to demonstrate and stimulate new ideas for the benefit of the tenant farmers.

The Acton family still live at Acton Scott Hall, which was built circa

1580. It was one of the earliest buildings in the county to be built of brick. The grounds include two walled gardens, three lodges, an archery ground and a yew hedge 150 yards long.

At the turn of the century a wheelwright, blacksmith, carpenter and watchmender all worked in the village. Coffins were made in a shed behind the present telephone kiosk.

Of much earlier origin were the traces of a building discovered when the road to Hatton was straightened in 1817. It was identified as Roman but the excavation was never finished and was finally covered over and returned to agriculture.

Adderley ✤

There was a Saxon manor in Adderley before Domesday, and in the Middle Ages Adderley was bigger and wealthier than Market Drayton. Yet in this one parish two families vied for precedence in a feud which lasted down the centuries: the Corbets of Adderley Manor and the Needhams of Shavington.

Insults were regularly exchanged. The road from Shavington to Adderley church crossed two Corbet fields and was little more than a cart-track, but at one stage the Corbets actually laid a hedge and ditch across it to make travelling to church difficult for Shavington inhabitants.

In the 17th century the Needhams had their own private chapel built at Adderley church, to the anger of the Corbets. It was not till the end of the 18th century that the two families learned to live amicably in the parish. Today the Jacobean chapel, in startling contrast to the plain Georgian church rebuilt by the Corbets, stands as a reminder of what jealousy and pride can do to a community.

Alberbury ✤

Situated within ½ mile of the Welsh border, the village dates from the 12th century when Fulke Fitzwarren erected a castle, now a ruin, to guard the border country. Within a mile of the castle was an abbey. The abbey, the 11th century chancel in St Michael's parish church, the village school and a farm nearby were the property of All Souls College, Oxford. Sadly, in the late 1960s the school was closed and sold.

In the 1800s the village boasted many more dwelling houses than today. There were lime quarries in the neighbourhood, providing considerable employment, there was a large staff at Loton Park, home of the Leighton family, and of course many men were employed on the farms in and around Alberbury. It is estimated that there were approximately 70 cottages in the centre of the village but these have disappeared. Comparatively little development has taken place this century. Most people travel from the village for employment, other than the few still engaged in agricultural work.

Alberbury's most famous son was Thomas Parr the 'olde, olde, verie olde man' whose life spanned the reigns of ten Kings and Queens of England, and whose remains are interred in Westminster Abbey. He died, aged 152 years, while on a visit to London at the request of the King who wished to meet this famous old man. It was said that, having been accustomed to simple country fare, the high living at the Palace proved too much for Thomas' constitution. Legend has it that Parr did penance in his nightshirt, tied to the old sundial in the churchyard at Alberbury, after he had fathered an illegitimate child when he was well over 100 years of age.

All Stretton 🏵

Few places can have such a setting, between the Long Mynd on the west, sloping down to the edge of the village, its valleys or batches leading up to great stretches of bracken, heather and whinberry, and Caer Caradoc to the east with its distinctive rock formation and hill camp. On the flat land between the hills All Stretton has grown up. It is no picture book collection of rustic dwellings but a vigorous community that has built homes according to need and the materials available.

Although near to Church Stretton the village has a strong independent life. The children have never had a school here, generations of them have trudged, ridden or bussed into Church Stretton, but the village has its own post office, shop, pub, village hall, and church.

Opposite the All Stretton Stores is the Yew Tree inn, one of the oldest local buildings. It dates back to about 1620 and the ground plan shows that it may have been built as an ale-house. It offers a warm welcome to all, as it must have done for years. In thirstier times, notably while the railway was being built, there were five inns in the village.

The church of St Michael and All Angels, built in 1902 as a daughter

St Michael and All Angels, All Stretton

church to St Lawrence in Church Stretton, has made local ecclesiastical history as it is now a 'shared building' with the local URC congregation.

A proportion of retired people live here, but young families too. There is only one farm now actually in the village, though nearby farms also provide employment. People go to work in Church Stretton, in shops, hotels, rest homes, as builders or at the 'Pop Works' (Mineral Water Works). They commute to Shrewsbury, Telford and further afield.

Alveley 🌿

Alveley is a thriving village community in the south of the county, lying equidistant from Bridgnorth and Kidderminster, on the A442. Its history dates back to AD50, when the village consisted mainly of forest, bogs and stagnant lakes, and at this time it was called Forest Coed.

Alveley contains a wealth of evidence of its past, particularly the historic centre of the village, which comprises a variety of Grade 2 listed buildings, preserved to their original character and design. There are two churches – the Methodist Chapel built in 1862 and St Mary's parish church, which was built in 1140 of local red sandstone.

Also in the historic centre of the village is the Three Horseshoes Inn, built in 1406. This is in fact the oldest public house in Shropshire. The Bell Inn is another of the oldest buildings in the area. It is said that Oliver Cromwell once stayed the night at the inn, leaving his horses in the church vestry. The Bell Inn is thought to have been built initially from the rubble of an ancient Saxon church. It contains 18 to 20 carved stones, the exact origin of which remains a mystery but which were probably imported by the Vikings. Many of today's village societies hold their meetings in the old Malt House, adjacent to the Bell Inn. The Malt House was once used by the monks as a brewing place.

It was in 1349 that the Black Death struck the village, killing two thirds of the inhabitants, mainly men. The Butter Cross, a 6 foot stone pillar, which lies approximately one mile out of the village, is probably a reminder of this grim part of Alveley's history. It was here that produce was exchanged with neighbouring villagers, rather than risk taking the disease into other areas.

Much of Alveley's more recent history and indeed the principal employment of the area, has been associated with agriculture, stone quarrying and mining. The Alveley grindstone quarry, with its exposures of special red sandstone, has been identified by the Nature Conservancy

Council as a site of special scientific interest. Many buildings of the village were built from this sandstone. Elm Cottage, built in 1672, is an example, having walls which are 3 feet thick in places.

Alveley colliery was an integral part of the village until it was closed down in 1969. It did leave behind its spoil tips, which are now being converted into a Country Park, overlooking the Severn Valley and its famous railway.

Annscroft 🌿

Annscroft is a roadside settlement about 4 miles south of Shrewsbury on the Longden–Pulverbatch road. Christ Church was built in 1869 and the roadside cottages were occupied by farm workers and miners from Moat Hall colliery, which closed in 1953.

There was a small shop, and Mr Bunn, the baker supplied bread and confectionery. A descendant of the original Mr Bunn still lives in the village. There are no business establishments in Annscroft now, and the nearest shop and post office is at Longden.

The present population emphasis in Annscroft is on younger, business people with school age children attending Longden, Pontesbury and Shrewsbury schools.

The road through the village has been widened with a pavement on one side – a necessity to cope with the numerous cars commuting to Shrewsbury and beyond. It is a world away from the days one elderly lady recalled when she always threw her cottage rugs onto the road early in the morning, where she brushed them vigorously. This action set up a daily pantomime when the wife of one of the smallholders walked her cows through the village after milking. Their verbal exchanges were highly enjoyable to their neighbours.

Ash 🌿

Like so many other villages, Ash takes its name from the woods which once covered the county. Ash and oak were then to be found in plenty.

Ash Grove, now the Lady Lambert Nursing Home, was once the centre of village activities, the house and lovely gardens on many occasions being the setting for church fetes etc.

For a good family walk there is Brown Moss, 80 acres of heathland,

15

with a large sheet of water, bog areas, woodlands and an abundance of plant life and birds. Many years ago it was common land. The smallholdings on the perimeter had grazing rights and their cattle, horses, sheep and goats kept the undergrowth under control. The manorial rights were purchased by the County Council and they are the caretakers of this Nature Reserve.

Ashford Carbonell
& Ashford Bowdler 🦔

Ashford Carbonell lies 2½ miles south of Ludlow, and with its neighbour across the river Teme, Ashford Bowdler, is one of the most southerly parishes in the county of Shropshire. The names Carbonell and Bowdler are derived from Norman landowners. On leaving the A49, the village is approached by crossing firstly, the railway bridge, and then the ancient Teme Bridge.

On entering the village, there is an avenue of young chestnut trees, planted to commemorate the Queen's Silver Jubilee in 1977, and a handsome Victorian stone school building dated 1872.

The little Norman church of St Mary Magdelene is surrounded by yew trees thought to be over a thousand years old. The church is particularly noted for its beautiful arrangement of windows at its east end, and contains a very unusual vesica window.

Opposite Church Lane is the lane leading down to Teme's Green, the site of the original ford after which the village is named. This is often used for summer picnics though care must be taken when bathing or paddling. Just upstream is Ashford Mill with its very fine horseshoe weir up which salmon can be seen leaping in autumn. An Ashford Mill is mentioned in Domesday Book.

The village street is a pleasant mixture of architectural styles. In the past, it was part of a coach road from Ludlow to Little Hereford and on to Tenbury Wells. The funeral cortège carrying Prince Arthur, eldest son of Henry VII, was thought to have used this route on its way to London. Now, however, there is no vehicular access beyond the county boundary. The road forks at the end of the village, passing each side of the small green where a walnut tree was planted to commemorate the Queen's Coronation in 1953.

16

Aston Eyre 🦢

Lying sleepily in a small hollow one mile west of Morville on the B4368 road, Aston Eyre is a tiny hamlet with much history attached to it. At the time of the Domesday Book, its name was Estone (East Town) and so remained until the end of the 13th century when it became Aston Eyles, getting the second part of its name from the Aers who owned the manor. The centre of the hamlet consists of an attractive half-timbered farmhouse, a church and the old manor house and gatehouse.

The tiny church, perched above the road and surrounded by daffodils in spring, was built as a chapelry to Morville church in 1132. It is unusual in that it is not dedicated to any saint. Above the south door is a Norman tympanum depicting Christ's entry into Jerusalem. It is almost certainly of the same date as the rest of the building and has been described as the best of its kind in Shropshire. It had some sympathetic restoration by the staff of the Victoria and Albert Museum during the 1970s.

Behind the church, stands the large building which was the original manor house. Now used as farm buildings it was a residence of much importance with a great hall and many other chambers, lit by mullioned windows. In front of it, although extensively added to, stands the gatehouse, now a private residence, which is of a similar age.

Over the years Aston Eyre has become much smaller. The census of 1841 records the population as 130, now it is home to only 50 inhabitants. Farming is the sole occupation carried out in the parish and as the need for labour diminished due to mechanisation, so the numbers dwindled.

Aston-on-Clun 🦢

Aston-on-Clun, so called because it is east of the Clun, was referred to as Eston in Domesday and was part of the Manor of Hopesay. Situated in the peaceful Clun valley, the village has a bustling village shop and post office, the Kangaroo Inn which is the only inn of this name in England and the Forge Garage, so called because it was originally the blacksmith's shop where horses were shod and farming implements repaired. The blacksmith is still living in the village. It was he who gradually turned it into a garage when tractors came along and with them the motor car.

Where once was the village green, stands an English or Native Poplar some 250–350 years old and which has been quite hollow for 100 years or more. This is the Arbor Tree which on Arbor Day, 29th May each year, is dressed with flags, originally flags of the Commonwealth but these days, although trying to stick with tradition, a few other flags are given. The flags are displayed to commemorate the marriage on 29th May 1786 of Mary Carter of Sibdon, to John Marston of Aston-on-Clun. The tree leans with the prevailing wind but it is quite safe and produces good foliage.

There are two round houses in Aston, believed to have been built by an eccentric during the period 1750–1830. One next to the Kangaroo Inn seems to have survived without too much alteration to its external appearance.

Some Ludlow historians have recently discovered a deserted village in the field behind the village hall and in certain light and grass length conditions the outline of a street and cottage mounds can be seen.

On the outer boundary of the village at Little Brampton crossroads is a stone built signpost of great antiquity with perforated iron arms.

Atcham 🌿

The name Atcham is a shortened form of Attingham which itself represents 'The House of the Children of St Eata'. St Eata, the patron saint of the village church (the only existing dedication of that name) lived in approximately AD650, and formed a small community at a ford of the river Severn some miles south east of Shrewsbury.

The church is first mentioned in 1075 and the village has continued in varying forms until the present day. It now houses some 180 parishioners and is in the midst of a strong farming community.

The busy A5 trunk road runs through the village and the main landmarks at Atcham are the two bridges over the river Severn. The old stone bridge was designed by John Gwynn (1769–76) and the new concrete bridge by Salop County Council in the late 1920s.

Sadly, the village school is now closed and the younger children go to Upton Magna school, some 3 miles distant. Older children travel in to schools in Shrewsbury or Much Wenlock. The post office now only functions on a part-time basis but the village store and garage open at normal business hours.

The village is to some extent dominated by Attingham Hall, designed in 1875 by George Steuart for the first Lord Berwick. It is now the property of the National Trust and a very considerable tourist attraction. The grounds, designed by Humphrey Repton, house many beautiful trees and a deer park. The Mytton and Mermaid Hotel in the centre of the village was once the Dower House of the Attingham estate.

In 1926 Lord Berwick presented to the village, as a war memorial, the Old Malt House, a handsome red brick building in the village. Thanks to a very active committee, this now serves as a village hall and is the focus of many activities. There is a popular and well attended Atcham Club and a new and promising Bowling Club.

Barrow 🌿

There have been many variations on the name of the village, Barwe and Barewe being just two.

The church of Barrow is dedicated to St Giles. The chancel is the oldest part of the church, a chapel was built here about the 8th century. In 1663 a great deal of repair was needed to the church due, no doubt, to the neglect it had received during the Commonwealth. In the churchyard is a cast iron monument dated 1807, a reminder of local industry.

One person buried in Barrow in 1809 was Thomas Turner, who set up with a partner at Caughley and produced the beautiful china for which Caughley is famous. Caughley is part of the parish of Barrow. In 1799 Turner retired and sold the works to John Rose, who in 1814 closed the Caughley works and set up his own works at Coalport. Also in Barrow is the grave of Tom Moody, the most famous whipper-in of hounds in the 1700s.

The almshouses and the school were founded by John Slaney in 1612. The almshouse was for 6 poor men or women. The school was for the teaching of 20 poor children. A sum of £10 a year was left towards the cost of the schoolmaster. They were built at first on a hill overlooking Willey, but were moved to where they are today by the first Lord Forester.

The school at Barrow is still open although in the past it was feared it might go the same way as other small village schools. Today children travel to the school from Much Wenlock and Jackfield. Many people living in Barrow today are employed on the Willey Estate.

19

Baschurch 🦢

By the time of Domesday Book in 1086 Baschurch, the chief manor of one of the Shropshire Hundreds, with one of the few Shropshire churches, belonged to Earl Roger of Montgomery. His son gave it to Shrewsbury Abbey in 1101. In 1339 the Abbey tried to establish a new town with borough status in the part still called Newtown. This failed however and Baschurch remained a village with its 13 townships, some of which were lost in later centuries.

The Norman church was burnt down in a Welsh raid in 1404, but the south wall and lower part of the tower still retain some 12th century work. A few houses near the church are old timber-framed buildings. A Methodist chapel was built in 1873 in Newtown and there was until recently a Roman Catholic church.

Stanwardine-in-the-Fields was the birthplace of Sir Roger Acheley, a

The General Store, Baschurch

20

draper and Lord Mayor of London in 1501. Boreatton Hall (Elizabethan) was the home of Sir Thomas Harris, leader of a plot in March 1655 to seize Shrewsbury Castle and town in the Royalist cause. Boreatton Hall was afterwards purchased by the Hunt family, whose most famous member was Dame Agnes Hunt, who started a hospital in Baschurch, mainly for consumptive and orthopaedic patients. Finally this hospital became the renowned Oswestry Orthopaedic Hospital.

The railway came to Baschurch in 1847 and cattle auctions and a Friday market for corn, butter and poultry were soon established beside the station. The Boreatton Arms, 'a commodious inn' and posting house, with 17 horses, was built by the station and licensed in 1851. The smaller Admiral Duncan, on the main road, dates from the late 18th century, while the small New Inn near the church is mid 19th century.

There is much new housing, and it is still the largest village in an agricultural area. Many of the inhabitants of the village are retired. Of those who work, most commute to jobs outside the village – Shrewsbury is only 9 miles away. There is no railway station now, but there is a bus service. Much shopping is done in towns, but Baschurch still has its village shops.

Bayston Hill ℘

East of the A49 is the common, flanked by the former Victorian Christ Church, a vast vicarage and school, all with new uses, and a variety of old and modern dwellings. The old school now bears the name of Mary Flavel, a local benefactress.

The A49 through Bayston Hill once had 12 pubs to serve the thirsty drovers, several shops, a craftsman's workshop and two cobblers. Three pubs still remain. In a nearby Sharpstones Lane cottage, an old 'coffin chute' can be seen, as the stairs were too narrow for the purpose.

Lythwood Hall was designed by George Steuart of Attingham Hall fame and built over 200 years ago for the village squire. Some older residents still remember Lythwood Road as the Coach Road and refer to the Coach House. They recall children's Christmas parties and soup for the poor provided by the last squires, the Hulton Harrops. A local builder's daughter saw the graves of horses and dogs in the Hall cellars, which had to be filled in when the Hall was converted into flats.

The library is named after Mary Webb, the novelist and poet. This eccentric lady lived a while at Spring Cottage, on Lyth Hill, overlooking

21

the beautiful Stiperstones and Shropshire hills which are the settings for her novels.

Three interesting buildings are still inhabited on Lyth Hill. The windmill, retaining its original structure but minus the sails, were built in 1835 for local corn grinding and the preparation of flax for the industry at nearby premises still known as the Rope Walk. Here ropes were made for the lead mines and collieries, including Upper and Lower Pulley. Great Lyth Manor, recently restored to its former beauty, was built in 1638 to replace a timber-framed building held by Roger the Huntsman in 1086. After 1948, when it became derelict for some years, tales about this haunted house abounded among the locals.

This is a place of contrasts, where an ancient settlement and forest changed to open farms and shallow coal mines and in the last 25 years has become such a large busy modern village, that some call it a satellite of Shrewsbury.

Bedstone 🌿

Bedstone is a small village near the Powys and Herefordshire borders, 6 miles south east of Clun. At the time of the Domesday Book, it was known as Betieteune. It is an attractive village, set among many trees and backed by hills.

The farm and many of the cottages are still part of the Ripley estate, the owner of which is Sir Hugh Ripley. The Ripleys moved to Bedstone from Yorkshire in 1870. Bedstone Court, built for them, was a calendar house, with 365 windows. This was one of the first houses in the area to have electricity. There was an estate sawyard and a wheelwright and blacksmith in the village. At one of the cottages, named appropriately Laundry Cottage, all the laundry for the Court was done.

Bedstone Court is now a college. This means, of course, that during the termtime, the village population is greatly multiplied, and the college has a considerable impact on the area.

There was a chapel erected in Bedstone in the time of Edward the Confessor. The present church, St Mary's, is a small Norman church with a Saxon font. The small tower, a more recent addition, is partly half-timbered.

The original Manor Farm house was built about 1350. It has a cruck hall with added box-framed cross-wings. The central truss of the hall survives. At one time, the farmhouse was converted into 3 cottages. The datestone E.I.B 1755 above the front door indicates the date of more recent alterations and the stone casing of the hall.

There was a school in the village, which opened in 1750, until about 1947. It has now been converted into a very attractive private house. Nowadays, the children travel to the village school at Bucknell, 2 miles away.

There has been a village shop in Bedstone for over 100 years. This was originally managed by the Satie family, and continued by the Morris' from the Corve Dale, one of whom married a Satie daughter. The shop originally stocked groceries, but nowadays sells only sweets, chocolate, soft drinks and cigarettes. The post office too is of longstanding and was first opened in 1908.

Berrington 🌿

Berrington church is built on Saxon foundations and the oldest and most treasured monument is a 14th century figure of a cross-legged knight carved from a solid piece of oak. The story goes that this knight was betrothed to a lady who lived at Eaton Mascott. He discovered that she was being unfaithful and decided to kill her. On the way he met a wild boar which instead attacked and killed him. The effigy of the boar lies at the feet of the knight. The local people call their knight 'ould Scrivven' or 'owd Scrivener' for some reason!

In Cross Houses stands the hospital. The Atcham Union Workhouse was built in 1793 and enlarged in 1871 and 1903. It was used as a workhouse until the First World War when it was converted to a Military Hospital. At this time there was a very busy little railway station opposite which brought the wounded straight from the Front. After the war, it became a General Hospital. In 1987 it ended its long and honourable career as a hospital and was converted to offices. The railway station closed in 1964, the rails were taken up and the 'cut' is now a thoroughfare for wild life. A thriving family of foxes patrol it frequently.

There are two public houses in Cross Houses, The Fox and The Bell. The Fox is probably the oldest building in Cross Houses, and was an old ale-house. A local lady remembers that revival meetings were held there from time to time. Every year a Harvest Festival is held in the Bell Inn, a tribute to this rural area. The produce is auctioned to customers and the proceeds go to local Senior Citizens.

Bitterley 🌿

The church, of Norman origin and restored in the late 19th century, contains an interesting font and an ancient chest. The most interesting feature is the excellent example of a Tabernacle or Market Cross standing to the south of the churchyard.

Beside the church is Bitterley Court, its front built in about 1700. Inside are beautiful Jacobean panelled rooms. At present owned by the Wheeler family it was formerly the home of the Walcotts, a family who were both squire and rector in Victorian times. Comparable with this house, in history and architecture, nearer to the A4117, is Henley Hall.

The village, with its sparse scattering of houses, rectory and school lies at a distance from the church. There is some speculation whether the cottages were moved when the Court was built. There is no shop or post office, but the village hall, known as Bitterley Hut owing to its original use as an army hut, provides a venue for village activities.

The school has a long history. From the 16th century there was a Grammar School here where Latin and occasionally Greek were taught. In 1874, losing its former glory, the school was classed as elementary and provided education for all and sundry, although it retained its title of Bitterley Grammar School until 1958.

Several of the large farmhouses in the area were once medieval manors in their own right and provide interesting examples of vernacular architecture. Upper Ledwyche for example, which had a church in the 13th century, conceals behind its plain brick exterior the hall of a 16th century manor house. Particularly interesting are the roof timbers and twisted Elizabethan chimneys.

Bedlam, or Titterstone village, as it now prefers to be called, presents the other aspect of the area. The parish itself extends to the summit of Titterstone, the boundary marked by a three-forked pole. Here, at a height of 1,750 feet, the ancient Britons once built a strong hill fort in a commanding position. Little trace of this remains, though the granite boulders and scree which form the Giants Chair are clearly visible and provide an excellent point from which to view the Welsh Borders and beyond. Titterstone is capped by a rock, known locally as Dhu stone, owing to its tendency to become 'Dhu' or black when exposed to the air. Underneath are layers of coal and ironstone, mined here in the late 19th century. The mining company intended to build a railway line from Ludlow to Titterstone, but owing to the steepness of the terrain, the railway terminated at Bitterley Yard and an incline was constructed, the full trucks going down providing the momentum for those going up.

Bomere Heath 🌿

The village was originally a large piece of open common land with a sheet of water in the centre in the form of a bow from which the name of Bomere Heath is derived – bow shaped mere on a heath.

In the early 16th century families began squatting on the common or heath lands. Here, unlike some other places, they were allowed to stay in the cottages they built, but a small fine was imposed which eventually became a rent.

In the 1920s Bomere Heath was still a hamlet, and the general water supply was restricted to just 3 public pumps. In dry seasons farm animals had to be driven to spring-fed pools, hence the practice of building farm houses near to spring water. From about the middle of the 1930s installation of modern amenities eventually transformed it into a true village with a modern school, block of flats and bungalows for the elderly.

There is still some common land nearby called Merrington Green, from where clay was taken for use at Leaton Brick & Pipe Works and Old Woods Brick & Tile Works, no longer with us. Previously a gypsy site, in the Second World War it was used as an American camp, and later as one for German prisoners of war. It has now been taken over by the Conservation Trust.

The village is surrounded by the farming community. The largest landowner is the Hon. Charles Bridgeman whose father the late Earl of Bradford bought the estate from the Lloyd family and who now lives at Albion Hayes, one of the oldest houses in the area. One of the farms follows the organic farming system, and retails its own flour and breakfast cereal under the name of Pimhill.

Bourton 🌿

A small, sleepy hamlet nestling at the end of the Corve Dale and close to Wenlock Edge. The village is approached from Much Wenlock by an avenue of horse chestnut trees which were planted to commemorate

Queen Victoria's Diamond Jubilee. They display pink and white candles in the spring and magnificent conkers in the autumn.

The church has superb views of Brown Clee Hill and has a lych-gate and yew trees, which generations of Bourton children have climbed after Sunday services. The church was a Chapel of Ease for the Bourton estate, and as such, was only licensed for marriages in 1957. The Manor, next door, had fallen into disrepair but is now renovated. The village school closed in 1969, and has been converted into a private residence. In the centre of the village is an old Elizabethan farmhouse, with a dovecote which can be seen on the side of the road.

There are fruiting cherry trees which were planted for the Coronation of Queen Elizabeth II, one for every child in the village at that time.

The mains water supply did not come to Bourton until 1981. Until then water was supplied from a borehole on the Bourton estate, and some of the outlying farms and houses are still supplied by borehole water.

The village has changed in the last ten years. Before it was basically an estate village with cottages and farms let on the Bourton estate, but more recently the houses in the village have been sold off as they became vacant, and are now in private ownership.

Brockton 🌿

Brockton is a small hamlet standing at crossroads on the Shipton to Much Wenlock road. It is partly in the parish of Shipton and partly that of Stanton Long. The school for the area is situated here but the old building built in 1845 is no longer used and the children now enjoy all the facilities of a modern school nearby. The Feathers Inn is a focal point.

The South family have been blacksmiths for several generations but with the demise of the horse the work now done is mainly ornamental ironwork. In addition they have also run the post office.

Bromfield 🌿

In fields surrounded by golden broom Bromfield was founded, settled between the confluence of two rivers, the Teme and the Onny. Bromfield was mentioned in the Domesday Book of 1086, and long before that Roman battles were fought in the area. Burial mounds (known as tumps) can still be found at the well known Ludlow racecourse.

The church at Bromfield has always played a major part in local life. A Royal Charter dates from Edward the Confessor and the secular canons were quite famous. A Norman church replaced the Saxon one and in 1155 the canons transferred to a Benedictine Priory.

Bromfield once had a landmark of great interest – 12 poplar trees transported by stagecoach from London and planted to commemorate the birth of Louisa Florential Hodges in 1822. She was the 13th child of the Rev Thomas Hodges and lived to be 93 years old. These poplars were known locally as the Twelve Apostles and curiously one of the trees fell on a Good Friday. The remaining trees were damaged by gales and in the early 1900s 12 more poplars were planted, 11 by the old road bridge and one in the estate yard, but this one never flourished. They came down in 1968.

At the turn of the century gypsy families often camped on the sands by the river. Horse-trading took place, babies were born and on one memorable occasion a wedding took place. The village ladies supplied the food, cake and veil for this gypsy wedding and it was a very colourful event at the time.

All but three of the properties in the village are owned by the 14th Earl of Plymouth who lives at Oakly Park. Most of the inhabitants depend upon the estate for their livelihoods, working on the land, the forestry, office or workshops.

Broome ✍

Years ago this was a small village with only a farmhouse and several workmen's cottages. It had a local inn and quite a busy railway station. Around the 1870s the South Wales Railway line was doubled and lots of workers swelled the community. The local inn was named the Railway Inn, though originally it was called the Engine and Tender and recently it has resorted to that name and now caters for tourists and caravans in summer.

The station was quite a busy place and boasted a station master, clerk, porter, warehouseman and signalman. Houses were built for these men in Railway Terrace with the station master's house opposite. The station yard was very busy, having two coal wharves, a large warehouse and cattle pens and a large timber yard.

The oldest house in Broome is the Old Forge, said to have been mentioned in the Domesday Book. It has three pairs of cruck timbers and some walls are wattle and daub, a rough framework interlaced with wickerwork and covered with plaster or clay to form a wall. The same family have lived in this house for at least 200 years.

The station is now demoted to a Halt on the Central Wales line running from Shrewsbury to Swansea. Certain trains can be joined by a frantic waving of hands as the train approaches and of course if returning to Broome, it behoves a passenger to tell the driver before getting on the train – or else!

Broseley & Benthall ✎

Medieval Broseley was called Burwardesley and was an important agricultural settlement but latterly became the original town of the Shropshire coalfield. At the time of the Industrial Revolution it was the largest parish south of the river Severn and included the hamlet of Jackfield. The principal iron foundries were at Broseley and Benthall where sophisticated parts for bridges and engines were made, also domestic utensils such as weights, frying pans, cider and wine presses.

The coal and iron trade started to develop in the 16th century and mines became of national importance. The ironmasters built themselves large houses in Broseley but it was possible for squatters to settle on common land and often these houses were enlarged into terraces and the number of dwellings multiplied out of control. Many of these cottages still survive.

John Wilkinson, well known for his involvement in the iron trade and who made the first iron boat and the first coal cutting machines, bought a house in Broseley. In recent years this has become a museum and houses the Wilkinson Collection. This house, The Lawns in Church Street, may later house the Broseley Museum also. After John Wilkinson left in 1800 he leased the house to John Rose, the china manufacturer.

The prosperity of the iron industry was shortlived but there was still an abundance of local clay and Broseley became famous for its clay pipes. It was the centre of pipe making almost from the time tobacco was first imported into Britain.

By the time the coal seams were exhausted, Broseley had an abundance of churches, chapels, a market and shops but these became surplus to requirements when people started to leave the area to find work elsewhere.

Benthall Hall is a 16th century house now owned by the National Trust, but still lived in by the Benthall family. Cecil Hill, whose family had traded in Broseley for 80 years, made about 70 new leaded lights and repaired others when restoration work was done. During this work he came across a light which had been made by his grandfather, Richard Hill, who then worked for Willey Estates, on which he had written with his diamond 'R. Hill, July 2nd, 1860'. Cecil Hill was asked if he would like to have the pane of glass so he replaced it exactly 100 years later to the day with one on which he wrote his own name and date.

Buildwas ♘

Buildwas is situated in the beautiful Severn valley, some 2 miles upstream from the famous Iron bridge. It is a small rural village, consisting of a small housing estate, several farms, a village hall and post office.

Buildwas Abbey was founded in 1135 and had an uneventful existence until the last abbot surrendered it to the king in 1536. However it is said that the ghost of a murdered abbot still haunts the ruins.

The village church is of medieval origin and was one of the possessions of the Abbey. The present church was rebuilt after a fire in 1720, with stones from the Abbey ruins.

The first local school for the children of poor families was built in the grounds of Marne Wood Hall at the beginning of the 19th century. The school remained open until the 1850s, when a county school was built.

Buildwas Bridge was designed by Thomas Telford and erected in 1796. The present bridge is a replacement, although the date plaque has been retained.

Bucknell ♘

Bucknell is situated in a valley between Coxall Knoll and The Mynd and between Leintwardine in Herefordshire and Knighton in Wales.

The church is in the middle of the village by the river Redlake. St Mary's church was built in 1140. The then Lord of Bucknell gave the church to the Abbot of Wigmore Abbey, for it seems he was charged with grave misdemeanours in King Henry II's court and could no longer remain in England!

In 1547 a schoolmaster was appointed to Bucknell. The Old School House still stands and since then has been a shop, a bakery, and now a dwelling house. The present school was built in 1865 and fortunately is still a thriving Church Primary School.

The railway came to Bucknell in 1865 and the station was a busy place

C. Heath.

Bucknell Village

with a full staff and manned level-crossing. A coal depot was established by the station and still operates today. The railway runs from Shrewsbury to Swansea. It had 2 tracks but with the Beeching cutbacks in the 1960s it was reduced to 1 track and the station unmanned. The line travels through Wales and is one of the most beautiful routes in the country, now referred to as the Heart of Wales Line.

Bucknell was for many years a self-contained village, having a post office and general stores, 4 pubs, a butcher, shoemaker, a smith, a wheelwright, a thatcher, an undertaker and a policeman and a corn mill. There was plenty of employment in the village. Nowadays most work is outside the village.

Burlton 🍂

The early years of this little settlement were stormy, with endless skirmishes amongst the English and Welsh, plundering and much land devastation. In 1349 came the Black Death which was severe in Shrop-

shire. Burlton is thought by some historians to have been amongst the settlements from which the inhabitants fled, re-establishing themselves a mile or so away.

Earlier this century there were 37 dwellings which included a pub, a post office, a shop and several farms. All were mixed dairy farms and all made butter and Cheshire cheese in the farmhouse. Pigs were kept as a vital link in the chain, to drink the whey, but almost all the cottagers also kept a pig in the sty at the bottom of their garden. Water was a precious commodity, pumped from wells possessed by very few householders. Farm work and transport was, of course, undertaken by horses, and this included haulage of coal and other heavy goods from Baschurch station or Weston Wharf.

Although most men were farm workers, the village was still fairly self-supporting and there were various allied trades, such as blacksmiths, wheelwrights and brewers. Others worked for the gentry as boot boys, gardeners, grooms, etc.

The estate was sold in the 1970s and now most people work outside the village. New houses have been built, but the post office, shop and smithy have been lost.

31

Burwarton 🌿

Burwarton is a small village halfway between Ludlow and Bridgnorth, on the eastern slopes of the Brown Clee. Burwarton has been in the ownership of the Boyne family for several generations.

St Lawrence's church, built in 1876 (adjacent to older ruins) was made redundant in 1976. The peal of 6 bells were re-cast and installed at Bishops Frome in Herefordshire.

Burwarton was claimed from forest and scrubland. Signs of old roads, often depicted by yew trees, and used by drovers to take stock to graze on Brown Clee, can still be seen.

Calverhall 🌿

The village of Calverhall is centred around a group of buildings including the almshouses, the church of Holy Trinity, the village hall and working-men's club, and The Old Jack Inn.

The almshouses, a chapel and a school, were originally founded in 1724 by Catherine Kerr. The rules were very strict. 'There must be no strong liquor, no cursing, swearing, pilfering or breaking of hedges'! It was stated that the children attending the school should be from the families of the poorer tenants and that they must work hard and attend chapel, otherwise they could be dismissed.

The Old Jack Inn is famous for 'Jack of Corra' which was a well known drinking vessel made of leather and was interesting as a relic of by-gone days. It is believed that a person named Corra or Kerr directed that any wayfaring traveller should call and refresh himself with the 'Jack', which should be filled with good malt liquor on the payment of one penny. The top and bottom of the vessel were encircled with a broad rim of silver upon which was engraved:

> 'From time immemorial
> Jack of Corra is my name
> Don't abuse me then for shame'

This cup was held and preserved at the Jack Inn but disappeared in about 1860.

In 1974 the village smithy closed and is now a private dwelling and garage premises. Mr Bill Jones, the last blacksmith in the village, made and presented a horseshoe to every local bride who married at Holy Trinity church.

There is no longer a school in Calverhall. The village post office also closed in recent years. However, many new people have come to live in Calverhall and the village hall is very well used. It is a meeting place for several clubs and is used for fundraising as well as many social events.

Cardeston 🌿

From the A458 Shrewsbury to Welshpool road, the visitor's attention is drawn to Cardeston by the unusual, octagonal church tower. The village is approximately 6 miles to the west of Shrewsbury, with a small group of houses in the immediate neighbourhood of the church, 4 farms and many scattered dwellings. A small stream, Cardeston Brook, runs through the present centre of the village.

Cardeston has altered both in size and in outlook over the years, largely as a result of changing employment patterns The village stands on the western edge of a breccia outcrop (Alberbury breccia) extending from Loton Park to Cardeston. It is known locally as Cardeston Rock. During the late 18th and early 19th centuries the stone was used extensively in many local buildings, including the church, Cardeston Manor and Cardeston House. The old quarry can still be seen alongside the Welshpool road. A limeworks, using stone from the quarry, was in operation between 1660 and 1817. Records show that in 1660, the lime produced was used in Alberbury church.

Approximately half the inhabitants of Cardeston now work in the towns of Shropshire and the West Midlands. This has broadened the outlook of the village considerably and brought in a wide cross-section of people with new ideas, opinions and tastes. Agriculture, however, remains a vital part of village life, as it has always done.

The church of St Michael was first recorded in 1276. An unusual feature is the barrel organ, made by T. C. Bates of London in 1850. It was acquired in the mid 19th century and can still be played. The church tower was added in 1844.

The church still observes the ancient services of Plough Sunday in January, when an old plough, originally horse drawn, is carried into the church and Rogation in May, when the parish bounds are marked.

Plough Sunday has, perhaps, a particular significance for Cardeston, as two members of a local farming family, the Smiths, have represented Britain in World Championship Ploughing Competitions.

Cardington 🌿

Bordering Apedale, this charming, historic village is tucked away among the hills of Willstone, Cardington, Lawley and the 1500 foot Caer Caradoc.

Nestling in the centre of the village, surrounded by clusters of old stone and half-timbered houses and cottages, lies the long-roofed part-Norman part-Gothic church of St James which is approximately 800 years old. Lying in the chancel is a magnificent effigy of Judge William Leighton, Chief Justice of Wales, who built nearby Plaish Hall. The legendary and elaborate chimneys of this superb Tudor house were built by a condemned criminal who happened to be a master-builder. He built them in return for his pardon but when they were finished the judge had him hanged from his own chimneys to ensure that they remained unique!

To the south east of the church is the Old Free School which is now a private house. This overlooks the Royal Oak, often referred to as one of the oldest licensed houses in England. Opposite the Royal Oak was once a ducking pool. The New Inn, which is now a private house, was in the past a brewery and a hemp yard where rope making was carried out.

Opposite the entrance of the church is a house known as the Maltster's Tap with an interesting barn which is a 1558 Shropshire longhouse, few of which remain in existence.

Also overlooking the churchyard is a house (formerly three cottages) known as The Barracks, where the troops attached to Judge Leighton's Plaish Hall were housed. Long since closed are the post office, village school, two shops, bakery, undertakers, pottery, and the blacksmiths.

Remote though the village is, it is fortunate to have two thriving coach companies which enable residents to commute in many directions and which also provide local employment on a large scale.

The village has changed over the years from a rural, chiefly farming, community to a more cosmopolitan one, which has helped to preserve the village by the careful and tasteful restoration of many old cottages and houses and the addition of a few new houses.

Caynham 🐾

The historic parish of Caynham lies on the southern slopes of Titterstone Clee Hill. It stretches from the valley of Ledwyche Brook in the south west, at a height of about 250 feet, to heights of over 1500 feet in the extreme north east. About half the parish is over 750 feet high.

The outstanding landmark in the south of the parish is Caynham Camp, a huge Bronze Age/Iron Age earthwork which occupies a site of more than eight acres. Excavations from 1959 to 1962 revealed evidence of occupation from about 1000 BC.

In the Middle Ages, Caynham was one of the many manors on the Welsh border belonging to the powerful Mortimer family of Wigmore. The most obvious survivor of the Middle Ages now is the parish church. One senses its antiquity as soon as one passes through the lychgate and along an avenue of ancient yew trees. Outside the church is an ancient cross, once used for preaching.

Farming has always been important in Caynham, involving all sections of the community. A 20th century farming cleric was the Rev J. D. D. Rider, a much loved and respected vicar from 1926 to 1959. He was known as the 'hunting parson', and is commemorated in a stained glass window in the chancel, which shows him walking to the church with a staff, with the village school and Caynham Camp in the background.

An important event of the 19th century was the building of the village school in 1834. It was a one room building of rough stone which was hardly altered until 1970. It can boast of being the first village school in Shropshire to be opened by the National Society, an organisation formed in 1811 to promote education 'to the principles of the Church of England'. It received a Government grant of £47 towards building, the first in Shropshire to benefit in this way.

During the 19th century the lower part of Caynham remained an agricultural area. Apples were widely grown and many farmers made their own cider. Most of the population however lived at the Knowbury end of the parish, where there were three public houses and two Methodist chapels. Caynham today has a population of just over 1000, but most of these still live up on the hill in Clee Hill and Knowbury. Like many rural communities, the southern part of the parish now has no shops, pub or post office, and many residents work in Ludlow, less than 3 miles away.

Chapel Lawn 🌿

The village is situated in the south of Shropshire, 5 miles east of Offa's Dyke. The wooded slopes of Hodre Hill, Brynheddin Wood with its magnificent broadleaf oaks and Caer Caradoc frame this unspoilt hamlet with its houses of local stone. The word lawn in the Middle Ages indicated a clearing in the woodland.

St Mary's church, made of local stone, stands proudly 530 feet above sea level. In the churchyard one very large old tombstone stands out from the rest. Permission was not granted for this to be erected and so determined was the vicar to prevent this that he made sure the gates were firmly locked day and night. However one dark night the youth of the area gathered to lift each stone over the wall and put it in the place it occupies today.

The school and schoolhouse were built in 1866 on the original village green. It was a very sad day for the whole area when in July 1985 the school was closed after months of campaigning to save it.

The Quern, a three-storey stone mill dating from the eighteenth century was functional until 1927. In 1600 Chapel Lawn Farm was built in black and white timber. Part of the house was used as a chapel and the peculiar chimney is thought to be the source of a tunnel crossing under the road to another farmhouse also called Chapel Lawn Farm.

The Woodhouse, with its delightful garden, was once the local hostelry and sweetshop. In 1886 it was known as The Woodcock Inn and an arrow on the outer wall states that it is situated 657 feet above sea level.

Chelmarsh 🌿

The parish of Chelmarsh covers a wide area and consists of a number of scattered hamlets. These include Hampton Loade, Sutton, Covert Lane, Spadeley, Astbury and the Common. Therefore there is no real definable centre. Its name mentioned in the Domesday Book was Chelmeres.

The two most notable buildings are the church and Chelmarsh Hall. The church was first endowed by Hugh De Mortimer in 1345 and the main part of the church dates from this time with later additions and modifications. The screen and the lychgate were carved by a local carving class at the end of the 19th century.

Chelmarsh Hall

Chelmarsh Hall was formerly a granary and was granted to monks in 1379 by Edmund Mortimer, Earl of the Marches. It was once connected to the church by an underground passageway which has now caved in. The Hall is now mainly Victorian with some late medieval doors and windows and fragments of a timber roof.

The main occupation of the village workforce was farming or mining. The mines being at Highley or Alveley, however, there was some open-cast mining on the Common, plus a shallow mine shaft (which is still visible) and its accompanying engine house which collapsed in 1984. The ghosts of miners can be seen walking down to the mine at certain times in the year.

The village was once a self-sufficient community. Two brothers, Albert and Tom Abbots, ran a mobile cider press, making cider for anyone with an orchard full of apples. Some apples were sent to Bulmers at Hereford. Damsons were also collected in large wicker baskets, packed on the train at Hampton Loade station, and sent to Manchester for use as dye in the cotton trades.

Furnaces were sited in Occupation Lane, where bricks were fired made from local clay. These were used to build three local farms.

The river Severn was crossed by a barge running on an underwater cable, which sometimes broke in heavy floods. Many a tale is told of boatmen and passengers going down the flooded river as far as Arley. One boatman known as the 'Water Rat' was renowned for getting people across the flood by using a punt to reach the ferry moorings.

Cheswardine 🐝

The first documentary record of Cheswardine is in the Domesday Book. It was then in the county of Staffordshire and called Ciseworde. The border now runs through Doley Mill Farm. Every approach to Cheswardine is a climb, as it stands on a hill with the Shropshire Union Canal meandering around the area. Five roads leading out to the west all cross the canal.

The parish consists of small hamlets, Soudley, Chipnal, Goldstone, Lipley, Hopshort and Park Heath. There was once a castle, but this has long since disappeared. The village is now dominated by St Swithin's church, which has a wonderful view of the Stretton Hills, Clee Hill and the Wrekin and at night a panorama of lights from Telford New Town.

The village is self-supporting. It has three inns, a garage and several shops, including a baker's shop with bread baked locally every day. The owner holds the recipe for the original Market Drayton Gingerbread.

Cheswardine Hall was built by the Donaldson-Hudsons in 1875. Col R. C. Donaldson-Hudson was the last owner. He was a great supporter of the Royal Salop Infirmary and after his death in 1941 a Pathological Unit was built in his memory. The Hall was eventually sold and became a Catholic College for many years. Later it was occupied by a school for maladjusted boys and now is a Residential Home for the Elderly.

Up until the Second World War the Curfew Bell was rung at 8 pm for 15 minutes every night from 5th November until 2nd February. Legend has it that someone lost in Bishop's Wood was guided to safety by the sound of the bell and requested that it should be rung every night at 8 pm. The old Church Charity, which at one time comprised of bread and flour given to anyone who was not the owner of a cow, is now paid out in vouchers annually. Wakes week, the first week in July, was a fun week, starting off with a parade through the village of Friendly Societies, a fun fair of Hobby Horses and other attractions, and several days of sport.

Chetton

Chetton lies south west of Bridgnorth, high on a spur of Brown Clee, at the end of a mile long cul-de-sac off the Bridgnorth–Ludlow road. The reputedly Saxon name means 'an enclosure of huts', and in the Domesday Book Catinton was said to be held by the Saxon Countess Godiva. The village itself is small, and when talking of Chetton, it is usual to include the hamlets of Tedstill, Eudon and The Down. The church of St Giles, probably established about 1086, has been re-built several times.

Cider Jack was one of Chetton's most famous characters. He lived in a cottage at Criddon, and did odd jobs in the parish. Drink was his undoing, and after scything the grass at The Old Inn for 10 shillings and a gallon of beer, he was mortified to find that he had already drunk the beer, and in fact owed 30 shillings for what he had drunk besides!

Chetton even has its own coal seam. Local people still recall going down a ladder to get coal from a shallow pit, and other villagers extracted it from local streams. Tedstill also had a brickworks.

The area has several timber-framed houses, including Eudon George, which has been restored by its owners. Nearby is The Down Mill, where the machinery was operating until 1947. An interesting tunnel exists under the road at Faintree. Chetton parish has two public houses – The Old Inn, reputed to be a former tithe barn, and The Down, formerly the Unicorn.

Chirbury

The village lies in a shallow valley on the borders of England and Wales. Wooded hillsides, arable land and meadows, a patchwork of many colours, form its picturesque setting.

In the early part of this century, the little grey stone and red bricked cottages housed many large families. The cottagers provided the labour for the nearby farms and the half-timbered Elizabethan Hall, standing just a short distance from the village.

Over the years some cottages have disappeared completely, others have been restored and modernised. New homes have been built, yet the population, which was 600 at the end of the 19th century, is now only 300. Farm mechanisation has reduced the number of workers needed on farms, young folk now commute to work in nearby towns.

The church of St Michael the Archangel, built on the site of an old Augustinian priory, was consecrated by Bishop Swinfield in the late 13th century. Remains of the old priory can still be seen in the churchyard.

A pathway across the churchyard leads to the school, an old grey stone building erected in the late 17th century. Looking at it from the outside it appears to be unchanged. Inside, the school has been completely refurbished, and here 30 children work in comfortable well equipped classrooms.

Adjoining the school is a half-timbered school house. It was here, in the late 19th century, under the roof, that one of the most important Chirbury treasures was discovered. This is the 'Chained Library' which can now be seen in the Shropshire County Library. These valuable books include some dating back to the early 16th century.

The village is skirted by the river Camlad. This is the only river which rises in England and flows into Wales, eventually joining the Severn. A stone road-bridge crosses the river at Whittery. Below the bridge is a cart track, along which many horsedrawn waggons laden with grain lumbered their way to Heightley Mill, now a mere shell.

Church Aston 🖋️

In the last century the biggest employer in the village was the Lilleshall Company. There were limestone pits near the Last Inn and the men were engaged in mining lime which was used for smelting at the blast furnaces at Lilleshall. In 1861 the mines were inundated with water, there were several fatal accidents, and all working ceased.

The first church was built in 1620 and was merely a Chapel of Rest. The present church was erected in 1867, dedicated to St Andrew.

In 1841 the Shropshire Union Railway line was built from Stafford to Wellington passing through the centre of the village. It was closed by Beeching in 1963 and much of the old line has been extended into gardens by residents living near the line.

Aston Hall was built in 1830 by Ralph Leeke who was lord of the manor and the village squire. In 1851 Mr Ormesby Gore MP lived there. He was groom in waiting to the Queen, deputy lieutenant of Shropshire, and a magistrate. He kept 11 servants including a coachman and groom.

The one inn, The Last, is about ½ mile from the centre of the village on the A518 to Wellington. In 1918 it was owned by two maiden ladies, the Miss Bolts, who scrubbed and cleaned the doorstep every day. No man was allowed in without wiping his feet and no swearing or spitting was allowed!

Claverley 🌿

Claverley is a picture postcard village approached by narrow, winding lanes on the extreme east of the county. Its half-timbered buildings and magnificent church attract visitors from far afield.

Roman legions camped here, followed by Saxons who built the first church. St Augustines's Lane marks the route taken by this divine during his mission. The Normans rebuilt the church and the world-famous frescoes were painted by 1200. Much time was spent in agriculture and forestry control as it continually encroached upon the settlement.

The Gatacre family lived here for a thousand years at Gatacre Hall. Many large houses were built using forest timbers – Powkhall, where Gladstone stayed when courting his bride Catherine Glynne of nearby Farmcote Hall; Ludstone Hall, a magnificent 17th century moated

Claverley Village

41

manor; 15th century royal hunting lodge Kings Barn; 18th century Dallicot Hall where Queen Mary stayed; and Chyknell, visited by Princess Alexandra.

Times and traditions have changed. May Day is no longer celebrated by the May Queen and attendants visiting houses in the carrier's cart collecting money. Midsummer Day used to be an exciting time with a procession, church service and great feast, the side-shows, swing boats and merry go-rounds continuing until late. On Empire Day the children had tea and sports at Chyknell, the highlight being the wagon ride home. Everyone helped to catch rabbits at harvest time and drunken pea-pickers created a nuisance!

Harvest festivals and auctions are still held in church and local hostelries and the Harvest Supper is popular. On Ascension Day the choir sing from the top of the church tower.

Clee Hill 🌿

Clee Hill stands some 1,749 feet above sea level, and overlooks the counties of Herefordshire, Worcestershire, Gloucestershire, Staffordshire and many more.

The view from the top of the Hill is varied and beautiful, and attracts numerous tourists during the summer months, who take advantage of the open common space for picnics and sightseeing.

Village life has changed considerably over the years. Local inhabitants from the small hamlets dotted about the area had to work very hard during the summer months to reap the harvest. Field grass was mown by horse-drawn mowing machines, and it was an arduous task turning the grass by hand and stacking it into tumps before housing it in barns for winter fodder for the animals. When the hay-making season finished field suppers were organised, and farmers' wives produced home made bread, fresh butter, cheese, pickles and cider.

The quarrying industry was established in the year 1860, when some 2,000 people were employed, and the stone produced was sent to many parts of the British Isles. The industry is still very buoyant today, but men now work in much improved circumstances. Other inhabitants travel to Tenbury Wells, Ludlow and Cleobury Mortimer.

Clee Hill village is well catered for with a variety of shops. The church is positioned in the High Street. There are two public houses also in the High Street, and dominoes and dart tournaments are held regularly. Clee Hill United have a good football team always placed well in the league table. Last, but not least, the village school is situated in Tenbury Road, some 100 pupils being educated to a high standard each year.

Clee St Margaret, Heath & Abdon 🐑

The small village of Clee St Margaret, the tiny parish of Heath and the scattered hamlet of Abdon are closely linked by narrow lanes and local interests.

Situated on the western facing slopes of Brown Clee Hill their skyline is formed by Clee Burf, Abdon Burf (which rises to 1772 feet) and the spur of the ancient hill fort of Nordy Bank. Commoner's rights below Nordy Bank are well-guarded by the vigilant Commoners Society.

Though there are no schools, shops, post office, pub, petrol station, sewage system, gas supply or street lighting, the villagers appreciate and feel privileged to be able to enjoy living in such an unspoilt, historically interesting corner of the county.

The isolated, unspoilt and simple Norman Heath chapel is still open regularly for services, though the parish has only 22 persons. There are clearly defined remains of a medieval deserted village in the field on the east side of the chapel and another next to Abdon's circular churchyard.

Clee St Margaret church was owned by the Hospitallers of St John until the 16th century. Unlike the lonely churches of Heath and Abdon, Clee St Margaret's church is right in the village of beautifully maintained cottages and gardens, which are regularly opened to the public.

Cleobury North 🐑

Cleobury North is a village nestling under the eastern slope of the Brown Clee almost mid-way between Bridgnorth and Ludlow. Until recently the village was entirely under the ownership of the Boyne Estates.

At the centre of the village stands the little Norman church. Adjoining the church is the Old Rectory which after ceasing to be used as a rectory became the home and surgery of the local doctor and has now been sold as a private residence. Opposite the church is Cleobury Court which for many years was the residence of the Hamilton Russell family.

On the eastern boundary is Mill Farm, which was mentioned in Domesday. A unique toilet is to be found here – a little building over a running brook! The adjoining premises are the Fisheries, originally run by Burwarton Estate and now a thriving private business.

To the south of the church can be found the village hall which was originally a granary over sheep pens. In the yard were the slaughterhouse and lambing pens which have now been demolished to make way for a carpark.

Adjoining is the Old Hall once the home of the Mytton family, now a shop, post office, and two houses. The only new buildings in the village are the retired people's bungalows.

Clive ✍

Clive is an exceptionally pretty village, most of the houses and the high walls, which are a particular feature of the village, being built of the local Grinshill stone in shades of grey, honey and red. The centre of the village is now a conservation area.

The most impressive building is the church, built on the side of the hill (or 'Cliffe' from which the village takes its name), the spire of which is a landmark from many miles away. Parts of the original 12th century Norman church can still be seen, and it was restored in 1849 and again in 1887. It is the Church of All Saints: the beautiful stained glass windows depict the male saints, with the carved wooden figures of the female saints holding up the roof!

Another fine building is Clive Hall, a 14th century building whose timber frame and herringbone brick is now hidden under stucco. The dramatist William Wycherley, author of *The Country Wife*, was born here in 1640, and his remains are buried in Clive churchyard.

The school was built in 1873 on the side of the hill. It is reached from the church via a steep and rocky path known as 'The Glat' – an old Shropshire word meaning a path or alley.

Some of the older houses of the village were built to house the quarrymen who worked the vast stone quarries on Grinshill. These quarries have been worked from Roman times, and the Roman town of Uriconium was built from this stone. It is a sandstone of unique construction, and can be seen in buildings all over the country. It even frames the famous doorway of 10 Downing Street.

Other cottages were built to house miners, for the copper mines whose vast tunnels extend underneath most of the village were also worked from Roman times. The main shaft is now enlarged to hold water which is pumped to supply cottages, houses and farms of the Sansaw estate, and it still produces 25,000 gallons each day.

Although the copper mines have been disused since 1886, and only a fraction of the former number of quarrymen are still employed in the quarries, Clive is very much a living village. Like every other picturesque village in England, it is now home to several retired people and commuters, but there are still many residents who work in the village. Most of them are employed in agriculture, but there are several small businesses in Clive, each employing several people.

Clun ☙

A Norman, Robert de Say, built Clun castle, now a ruin. Sir Walter Scott stayed in Clun and his novel *The Betrothed* is supposed to be set in the castle. The Duke of Norfolk owns the property, but the people of Clun enjoy the grounds at a nominal rent. A carnival and show is held there annually.

The Norman church will seat 600, and was extensively repaired in 1877 at the cost of £8,000. Trinity Hospital Almshouses were founded in 1614 by Henry Howard, Earl of Northampton. Twelve poor men of good character lived in individual homes. They were called to prayer by a bell and locked in at 9 pm each evening. They were given a cloak and hat and coal and tobacco at Christmas. Any money left over after their keep was to be spent on children's education.

The hump-backed bridge is most picturesque. There is a saying 'You be wiser when you've crossed Clun bridge'. Whether this is due to the trading abilities of the townsfolk or the narrowness and difficult angles to negotiate is a moot point! The parapet is damaged frequently.

Clun is a self-contained community. Last century the meeting place was the Assembly Room in the Castle Inn, then the Temperance Hall (1870) which held 200 people. 'The Hut' was built as a First World War memorial and lasted until 1979 when the New Memorial Hall replaced it. The story is that 'The Hut' sank at one corner, as it had been built over a buried cow!

Local agriculture has changed little over the years, except for becoming more intensive and highly mechanized. For example, on one large farm ten working horses used to be kept, plus ten young ones for replacements, and a large herd of Welsh Mountain ponies ran on the 1400 foot hill. Now the only horses kept are thoroughbreds for riding and racing.

There are no longer any milking herds in this district. Beef production and breeding English/continental cross cattle is the present fashion, and in this hill country sheep farming is the most popular way of life. The Clun Forest breed is chiefly kept, practical animals with black faces, good bones, meat and wool, ideal for crossing with other breeds.

Clunbury 🌿

Nestling at the foot of Clunbury Hill, ¼ mile from the main road which runs through the Clun valley, the peace of the village is usually only broken by the sound of residents' cars and the daily bus to Craven Arms and Ludlow. And, surprisingly, in view of the fact that over the past years Clunbury has become increasingly a retirement village, by the sound of children's voices, for it still retains its school. Though most of the children are now bussed in from the surrounding area the church school remains very much a part of village life.

Clunbury Hill, with its whinberry slopes, its sphagnum moss collected by the sackful in the early part of the century for dressing wounds, and its prehistoric stone upright marking the boundary between Clunbury and Clungunford, dominates the village and provides a dramatic backcloth to the houses beneath.

Although Clunbury was once an important Saxon development the oldest building which remains is the Norman church of St Swithin with its great Norman font and its sturdy tower – early 13th century but with signs of Jacobean restoration.

Though it has lost many of its older houses, replaced by more modern ones, still several late Elizabethan and Jacobean, half-timbered and with a wealth of beams, stand around the main street. It once boasted two chapels, but the only one remaining has long been turned into a house.

A mile away, still within Clunbury's postal district and partly within its parish boundary lies the hamlet of Twitchen, once a far more important settlement than it now appears. The name Twitchen means a 'fork in the road' and it is here that the old possibly Roman road to Clunbury is crossed by the 3000 year old Clun–Clee Ridgeway. This important highway ran from the hills of Wales to the coal mines on the Clee Hills. The museum at Clun contains many flints found along the route of the Ridgeway in Clunbury parish and as no native flint occurs in the area these point to the constant traffic along this road in prehistoric times.

Clungunford 🌿

When Gunnas the Saxon laid stones in the river Clun to make a ford he provided not only access to the west and Wales, but gave the village its name. The ford was replaced by a bridge in 1657, and a new bridge built in 1935. Under this the stones of the ford are still visible and some local people still call the village 'Gunnas'.

The Saxon settlement had a church and four outlying farms – Abcott, Beckjay, Coston and Shelderton. The Normans added to the village a manor house and a mill, and also built a motte and bailey castle as a defence against the Welsh raiders. The motte can still be seen just north east of the church. The wooden church was rebuilt in stone in the 13th century with its accompanying priest's house. Both the priest's house and a thatched cottage of similar date at Beckjay are privately owned and beautifully maintained.

The village had an ancient custom by which the parson provided a feast of bread, cheese and ale in the church on Easter Sunday for the poor and elderly. In 1636 the rector discontinued the custom so the angry parishioners petitioned Archbishop Laud to restore it! But he refused.

Clungunford also looked after its younger inhabitants. At least as far back as 1658 several fields were bought and the income used to help with the children's education. For many years the children were taught in a chapel in the parish church. In 1853 a school was built which flourished for about a hundred years.

The Manor House was demolished when Clungunford House was built in 1828. This is a Georgian mansion with a colonnade and has been the home of the Rocke family since its completion. The Rockes became squires to the village and employed most of the population either in the house or on the land. A hundred years ago the village cobbler, tailor, seamstress and miller lived in Tradesmen's Row – a line of cottages between the church and river, and on the site of the present Parish Hall was the smithy and wheelwright's shop. The post office and general stores in the village supplied most needs, with the baker, butcher and laundryman from the larger village of Leintwardine making deliveries by horse and trap.

Clungunford is only 4 miles from Wales and Welsh surnames are still encountered in the village, but its character is English rather than Welsh. There are about 150 residents, most of them involved in farming or retired people from other parts of Britain.

Coalbrookdale 🌿

This is where the Industrial Revolution began. In the 18th and 19th centuries it was world famous for its products – decorative tiles, Coalport china and cast iron. Here was erected the first iron bridge in the world. A great deal of information about the history of this World

Coalbrookdale Museum of Iron

Heritage Site has already been published and the Ironbridge Gorge Museum Trust tries to preserve and display as much as possible at several sites in the area.

The wooded slopes around the village are dotted with houses, which were built using local bricks and tiles of various colours, and the riverside walks and gardens attract many visitors. The oldest home, built of stone in the 16th century was used as a hunter's lodge by the nobility of the day.

For nearly 400 years Coalbrookdale formed part of the Borough of Wenlock but it is now part of Telford New Town. Many residents once moved away to find better housing, as many homes were without water or sewerage. These are now preserved as listed buildings! It has become the fashionable place to live and the shops cater mostly for the tourists.

Families then were large and often inter-related, living in small terraced houses. The foremen lived higher up the hill than the workmen, while managers and owners lived in larger houses nearer the top. Ironbridge children, including Billy Wright who captained England in the 1950s, played football on The Slip, where subsidence had left a flat piece of ground. Coalbrookdale children had a flattened bit of factory waste known as The Cinder Hill. Home-made toffee could be bought from Sam Ball whose caramels were 5 for 1d, Murphy's made and sold pop, nettle wine was 2d a half bottle and Mrs Brown sold hot Horlicks for ½d a cup.

The Ironbridge and Coalbrookdale Co-operative Society had several shops and there were numerous grocers who delivered the weekly order. The butchers had their own slaughterhouses, there were bakeries, dairies, breweries, a gasworks, several chapels, banks, 2 cinemas, a drill hall and 10 schools. All have gone, though one primary school now uses the premises built in 1911 to house the County High School.

Cold Hatton 🐝

Mentioned in the Domesday book, by the 13th century Cold Hatton was the property of Lilleshall Abbey and it later passed to the family of the Dukes of Sutherland, who sold it in 1912.

The Duke laid out lanes, planted hawthorn hedges, sank wells and built red sandstone cottages, all facing south, with a front door only, and just two up and two down. The stone for these cottages was quarried less than a mile away at Cliff Rock, a wooded gorge through which runs the river Meese. This joins the river Tern just below the Nobridge ford, through which carts dragged the rock.

At one time every holding on the estate had a walnut tree, received by the tenants to commemorate the coming-of-age of a son and heir. The original trees have now died of old age, but nuts from them were planted, and a new generation is now bearing fruit.

At Cold Hatton now there is a thriving garden nursery, a motel with licensed restaurant, a busy boarding kennels for pets, and a public house, The Seven Stars. This hostelry was used by the drovers who, before its enclosure, used the common land to graze and rest overnight the shod beasts they were driving from Liverpool to London for slaughter. At the very old festivity of Cold Hatton Wakes Week, common ground was used as a circular race track, the high ground in the centre being the grandstand.

By the meadows at Cold Hatton Heath there is an unusual structure, locally known as a chutor house. It is a large brick kiln built to dry the flax that had been retted in the nearby river Tern. It is thought to be of older construction than the Duke of Sutherland-type cottage it adjoins.

Until recent times, the drinking water for that house and a nearby timber-framed cottage, now demolished, was an ever running spring, which was reputed to have curative properties. People would walk miles to collect a bottleful for a sick relative. Alas, it runs no more, due to the drastic deepening of the river some years ago, plus the Severn Trent ground water scheme.

Cold Weston 🌿

Cold Weston is a tiny remote village situated on the lower slopes leading to Weston Hill, a hill of over 1,000 feet commanding magnificent views.

There are, if boundaries are correct, but 10½ houses in the village, although one can never be certain of boundaries in this lovely hill country. One boundary runs through the middle of a cottage, the Cold Weston half to the west and the Stoke St Milborough half to the east. In the early 19th century the house served as a retreat for unmarried mothers. Records suggest that, during this particular period of its history, the occupants of this house when visited by a parish overseer, moved hurriedly from one half to the other in order to claim monies from whichever parish the overseer represented!

To the east of the village lie the huge hills of Abdon Burf and Brown

Clee, the highest of the Shropshire hills, and to the north and north east lie Heath, Corve Dale and Wenlock Edge. Until some 40 years ago the road – Skirmidge Lane – which runs through the village was 'gated' leading for some way over common land of bracken and furze to Stoke St Milborough. About the countryside here, fox, stoat and weasel, finch, wren and buzzard still live out their lives, not because but in spite of human intervention.

Cold Weston still has its tiny 13th century church and graveyard, possibly of Saxon origin, set beautifully among ancient yews and limes and firs. Now, sadly, deconsecrated, this is of major historical importance as the church of a much larger deserted village, deserted probably in the 13th or 14th century, the tumps of which are still visible in the fields 200 yards to the west of the church. Both the deserted site and the church are listed ancient monuments. Why the early village was deserted is one of the many, many mysteries of this border country. Was it plague, or battle or simply that it was no longer possible for the villagers to eke out even the meagre living of those days?

Colebatch ✺

The village of Colebatch is situated 1½ miles south of Bishop's Castle on the main road to Clun. It has 24 dwellings with a population of approximately 61 inhabitants.

The name Colebatch was taken from a gentleman named Lefwyn de Colebech, as far back as 1176. Colebatch was once part of the Bishop's Castle Estate, which included The Pines, farms, cottages, saw yard and blacksmith's shop.

The black and white cottage in the centre of the village is 14th century. This cottage was the Reading Room on the estate before it was sold in 1921. Congregational services were also held there. Originally it was believed to be the kitchen end of the Manor House which belonged to the Burton family of Longnor. The house on the opposite side of the road now known as Brookside was the Estate Office where the rents were paid on quarter day.

The villagers once supped their ale in either of the two Ale Houses, one called The Barley Mow, the other The Fleece. The buildings which were once the Fleece have now been renovated into living accommodation. While these alterations were being carried out a broken pottery mug was found built into the wall, this was believed to be a charm to stave off witchcraft.

At the end of the lane a mount is to be found. This is a Norman motte, one of a series of fortifications built after the Norman Conquest. Used as a look-out in case of invasion by the Welsh, it was manned by one constable and about 30 men, having a wooden hut on the top and a stockade around the bottom.

The village of Colebatch has changed little over the years, agriculture still being the main occupation. The saw yard is still in use as a woodwork and undertaking business, but gone are the days of the saws being driven by a large black steam engine.

Condover 🌿

Little is known of Condover prior to 1086, but it appears to have been an established settlement at that time. The discovery of the 'Shropshire Mammoth' bones will anyway ensure Condover's entry in the history books – the bones of an adult female and three young having been found during quarry working at Norton Farm.

Condover Village as seen from the Village Hall

The church of St Andrew and St Mary is mentioned in the Domesday Book, as is also a mill, and it would appear that the church is one of the few buildings which today still stand on the same site.

The medieval Manor House, (thought to be Church House, the timber-framed house beside the church) was replaced in the 1590s by Condover Hall which is thought by many to be the finest example of a Tudor mansion in Shropshire and still stands today much in its original design. It is now owned and occupied by the Royal National Institute for the Blind as a School for the Blind.

Condover's most famous son, and also a favourite of Queen Elizabeth I, was Richard Tarlton, a jester in the Royal Court. It was said that he could 'undumpish her (the Queen) in a trice'. Tarlton was a native of Pyepit, that area of Condover where the present school now stands.

A school was established in Condover in 1591, and was located in various places including the workhouse and the house known as School House. In 1880 the present school was built at Pyepits. The school yard was once the site of clay pits, the clay being used for the making of clay pipes for smoking, hence the name Pyepits or pipe pits.

Today's inhabitants have less dependency on the landowners around the village, and a census would show members of nearly every trade or profession, many with their own transport. For those still dependent on public transport, only the bus service still serves the community, the railway station having closed some years ago. Condover however has altered little over the last few centuries, except for some new building to one side of the village near the smithy.

Cressage

Cressage is one of the growing villages of mid-Shropshire, ancient in its origins, but now dominated by modern housing. It is situated beside the A458 road which links Bridgnorth and Shrewsbury.

The name Cressage is a derivation of the original Saxon name, Cristesac (Christ's Oak) and as a place name is believed to be unique. The original oak tree was one of several ancient oak trees in the village. It is said to have stood on the site of the present war memorial. The Lady Oak, or a sapling growing from it, still stands in a meadow north of the Shrewsbury Road. Between these two oak trees is the site of the ancient church dedicated to St Samson, now marked by a simple stone memorial. It is said that St Augustine may have preached in Cressage in the 6th century. Whether or not this is true a church of Saxon foundation served the village until 1841, when because of persistent flooding by the river Severn it was finally abandoned and pulled down. The new church, dedicated as Christ Church, was opened in that year – a time when the village had a population of about 300. The population long remained static, but in the last two or three decades the village has grown rapidly.

The village hall in Sheinton Road is in constant use by the many organisations which flourish in the village. A public house, The Eagles, serves the village and supports the local football team. The Old Hall Hotel is a well known local landmark, standing close to the river. Parts of the house, a listed building, are half-timbered and date from the mid 17th century although the site is believed to be that of a medieval manor house. Castle Mound is, as its name suggests, the site of an ancient motte and bailey castle which controlled the ford across the river close to where the bridge now stands.

Oak Tree Farm is the only farm actually in the village. It is now run by Mr Sydney Price's two sons. Mr Price has now officially retired but retains a keen interest in sheepdog trials. In 1987 he and his dog Davy won both the national and the international Supreme Championships and have many other awards as proof of their skill.

Crudgington 🐑

The small village of Crudgington is situated on a slight rise near the confluence of the two small rivers Tern and Strine and at a strategic crossing point of the main A442 Wellington to Whitchurch and B5062 Shrewsbury to Newport roads. It appears always to have been essentially a farming settlement on land of good quality, particularly when well drained. Mentioned in the Domesday Book, when it had four fisheries, the name was spelled Crugetone.

Some of the black and white houses are thought to date from the 17th century. Of particular interest is the (now extended) cottage of cruck construction which stands on the main A442 road. The former Methodist chapel is now a private house, but St Mary's church (a daughter church or Chapel of Ease of High Ercall), erected by public subscription in 1863, was reopened in 1970 after a period of closure.

From the Middle Ages Crudgington was in the ownership of the incumbent Marquis of Stafford or Duke of Sutherland as part of the Lilleshall estate. Rapid expansion of the village took place in the 19th century.

All the cottages had large gardens, and the ones along the lane known as Crudgington Green had a few acres of land. Along the Green today a few of these operating as smallholdings can still be seen, and of particular interest is a beautiful cottage garden of wide renown. Private purchasing of all properties began in 1912 upon the sale of part of the Lilleshall estate, when some buyers of the larger farms also purchased several cottages. Now the majority of dwellings in the village are privately owned. Only about half a dozen completely new private houses, and 10 council houses (some of which are now privately owned), have been built in this century.

In 1921 a farmers' co-operative, sending milk by train to London in the winter and making cheese in the summer, was set up near to Crudgington crossroads. It became a true Creamery, collecting only cream for butter making, when it was taken over by the Milk Marketing Board in 1935. Having undergone several expansions over the years the present imposing complex houses the Milk Marketing Board's Research and Development Establishment as well as a depot and packaging units trading under the 'Dairy Crest' logo. It still provides employment, full time and part time, for around 300 people from the village and wide surrounding area.

Farming, both large and small scale, is still most important, for although decreasing numbers of workers are employed directly on the land, the majority of local people are dependent upon or involved with agriculture-related operations.

Diddlebury & Westhope 🐚

The village of Diddlebury is one of historic interest. The settlement is very likely to have been an early one, because the churchyard was once round in shape which denotes that early Christians took over what was once a sacred pagan site. Before the Conquest, the church and land belonged to King Edward the Confessor. Ancient features of St Peter's church, include a north wall of very fine herring-bone masonry, a small Saxon window set high up in it, and some interesting fragments of Saxon stone sculpture set in the north windows.

Diddlebury has perhaps one of the most picturesque village centres of all, with its ducks and geese cavorting on the Diddle pond, old stone and brick farm houses nearby, and the church still dominating the scene, attracting numerous visitors each year.

Westhope is a small village west of the parish of Diddlebury. A unique village, everything, church, village hall, farms, cottages is all part of a private estate and has belonged to the Swynnerton Dyer family for hundreds of years.

The village has a delightful little church. It was built in an orchard, which in the spring is a mass of daffodils. It was probably built by some early Lord of Westhope Manor as a private chapel and it dates back to 1650. At the entrance to the church there is a huge yew tree which, it is said, was planted in the year 1200.

For such a small village there is a large village hall, and this is the focal point of village life. Villagers meet there for dances, whist drives, over-sixties club, rummage sales etc. The Harvest Supper is a big night in the village's calendar, when the women cook a delicious meal, followed by entertainment of some kind. At Christmas time the church is beautifully decorated and there is a carol service when different villagers read a scripture, then everyone is invited to Lady Dyer's home for tea and mince pies.

Ditton Priors 🐝

Ditton Priors is situated about 800 feet up the Brown Clee, the highest hill in Shropshire. The village has a long history and the people who live, and have lived, there are justly proud of their surroundings and heritage.

At the time of the Domesday Book there were 200 inhabitants and the village was called Dodingtone. It came under the control of Wenlock Priory. Between the 14th and 17th centuries the Lordship of the village changed, and so did the name from Dodington (spelled several ways) to Dodyton Prioris and so to Ditton Priors.

For many years a carrier's cart brought produce and passengers from Bridgnorth, some 10 miles away, and at Monkhopton bank the passengers had to get off and walk so that the horse could be led up. Seventy years ago it sometimes carried a barrel of herrings, fresh from port, and women stood in their gateways, carrying a cloth covered plate, to buy them at 1d a dozen.

At that time, when men had finished their day's work, they would help farmers get in their corn. Afterwards their wives would glean, the corn being used either to feed their chickens or taken to the mill at Middleton Priors. The flour was kept in pillow cases and used for baking.

In the early 1900s there was a quarry at the top of the Clee producing Dhu stone, which was used for building and roads. To move this very hard stone a railway was opened in 1908 carrying both freight and passengers. Previously the stone was moved down the incline, a very steep man-made slope by a rope railway. The railway ran between Ditton Priors and Cleobury Mortimer and in 1938 was closed to passenger traffic.

At the advent of the Second World War the 'Admiralty' came. This was an armaments depot for the Navy and brought about a change to the village. The trains, during the war years, ran so slowly, because of the explosive nature of the cargo, that the crew had time to get off on the outward journey, set rabbit snares, and on their return collect the catch! The railway closed completely in the mid 1960s.

Nowadays, after many businesses had previously closed, there is a revitalisation, and now there is a butchers, greengrocers, post office and general store in the village. There is a thriving industrial estate on the site of the 'Admiralty' which brings employment to the district. The 800 year old church still stands over the village, which is a guardian of all that is worthwhile in English village life.

Donnington

Donnington was originally a hamlet whose inhabitants were mainly concerned with farming. Walkers Ironworks came to Donnington by the 1860s and employed many villagers. Some were employed in nearby collieries, owned by Lilleshall Co., and some remained in farming.

Houses in the village were built by the Duke of Sutherland for his estate workers, and some of these distinctive houses are still to be seen. The Duke sold the property in 1917.

There is no C. of E. church in Donnington, but 2 Methodist or Baptist churches were built in the late 1800s. In the 1960/70 period an ultra modern Roman Catholic church was built. The only schools years ago were in Trench, near the old Glassworks, and in Donnington Wood adjacent to St Matthew's church. Now there is an Infants School and a Junior School in Donnington (but according to the boards at the gates they are in Donnington Wood!).

In the late 1930s Woolwich Arsenal was transferred to Donnington and became the Central Ordnance Depot. This meant a large influx of newcomers to this area. New houses had to be built for them. The Depot also, during and after the war, provided many new and different jobs.

There are now quite a few shops at the Parade, and one public house,

The Champion Jockey, named after champion jockey Sir Gordon Richards, who was born in Donnington.

Nowadays it is hard to find the exact boundaries of what was originally the village of Donnington, as Donnington Wood, Trench and Wrockwardine Wood surround it, with only the centres of roads now as the dividing line.

Dorrington

This compact village lies on the busy Shrewsbury to Hereford road, virtually halfway between Shrewsbury and Church Stretton. It is set amid well wooded undulating farming land with the beautiful Cound Brook running along the east side of the village carrying the waters from the Stretton Hills to the river Severn.

Buildings in the village go back to the 17th century. The black and white Old Hall, now a restaurant, was first recorded in 1679 and the Horseshoes Inn in 1734. Most of the houses were built before 1850 and very little development took place until a few council houses and flats were built after the Second World War. In the past 20 years around 50 more houses have been built in a number of small developments.

The Shrewsbury to Hereford Railway came in 1852 and the station was opened in 1853. Between this time and early this century the village began to flourish. There were 5 inns and ale houses. The Railway Inn (now the White House) also held regular cattle sales. The sheep and cattle were driven down from the neighbouring hills of Picklescott and Smethcote and other villages round about. The station was closed in 1958.

The village owes much to the Hope-Edwardes family of Netley Hall. Their interests in the village originated in 1826 when the Netley estates were expanded into Dorrington. The church, school and village hall (Hope Edwardes Institute) were all funded and built by the family.

Before 1845, when the church of St Edward was built the parishioners travelled to Condover to worship. It is said that the washing away of the bridge over the Cound Brook cutting off Condover church influenced John Thomas Hope of Netley to give the land and build a village church.

John Boydell, the engraver and print publisher, was born in Dorrington in 1719. As a result of his great success he became Lord Mayor of London in 1790. His most famous production was the series of Shakespearean engravings which appeared in 1803. He died in 1804.

The village amenities have changed with the disappearance of most of the old village crafts. There are however a post office and general stores, a butcher, two inns, a school, a fine restaurant, a garage and doctors surgery. Dorrington has absorbed the many changes over the years and has retained its pleasant peaceful rural atmosphere for today's population of just over 400.

Easthope 🦌

Easthope is a small rural village with a church and post office, situated 5 miles west of Much Wenlock and 10 miles from Bridgnorth. Midway between Larden and Lutwyche Hall in Mogg Forest is the celebrated British encampment called the 'Ditches'.

In 1916, 40 people were employed to maintain the Lutwyche estate. In 1952 the estate was sold off, with each tenant buying their own property. The Hall was sold and used as a boys school, before returning to private use.

There are 6 farmers in Easthope parish, other inhabitants being commuters and retired people. The children of the village up to the age of 11 attend Brockton school, after which they go to Much Wenlock Comprehensive School.

The Malthouse reveals a medieval hall constructed in the early 1300s and translated to form a second hall in 1450, being the only example of its kind in Shropshire of medieval cross-wing type of building, and of great architectural importance. It consists of oak timbers and red bricks, the bricks being made at Easthope at that time. The kiln of the Malthouse was fired with coke and used for drying corn.

Bricks made at Easthope were baked in a kiln in the field above the big trout pool, the clay being dug from the field. Finished bricks were transported by rail down Easthope Cottage Farm fields in front of the then Dower House and across the road. The bricks were used to build a number of local houses and buildings.

In 1936 a Halt was built at Easthopewood by the GWR for local people to go by rail to Much Wenlock and Wellington for shopping. In the 1920s coal was collected by horses and dray from Longville station wharf and it was said to be a common sound at 5 am to hear horses and dray coming along the Wenlock Edge.

Eaton Constantine 🌿

This village is situated on a south facing slope above the flood plain of the river Severn. It can be seen from a distance mainly because of the position of the church, which stands higher than the village.

The history and origins of the village are tied to Leighton and in 1242 Thomas de Constantin came from Normandy to be Lord of the Manor, thus giving the village its name.

The village consists of dwelling houses and farms ranging from 400 years old to modern. The most important house in the village is Baxter's House, built around 1645. It was the home of Richard Baxter, the Puritan Divine who became chaplain to Oliver Cromwell.

Opposite Baxter's House is a black and white thatched cottage, known as Wayside, which has a very interesting wall built of stones, said to have been carried to this area from the Lake District when the ice cap melted. There is a great quantity of this stone in the village and under hedge bottoms are walls built from it.

Eaton Constantine has seen many changes. It once had a village inn known as The Castle and unfortunately the village post office and stores have also gone.

The road runs through the village to Upper Longwood, which boasts a village pump. Two semi-detached cottages have the name The Warren, indicating that in medieval times the Lord of the Manor housed his warrener here for breeding rabbits for his table. At Upper Longwood you can turn left to Lower Longwood where the remains of brickworks can be seen. This area has also had opencast coalworkings and is known locally as the Coalpits. Or turn right and go past an ancient boundary stone to Neves Castle, which is not a castle at all. Its origins are lost in the mists of time, but there is a sizable mound which could have been the site of an old motte and bailey or an ancient British fort, lying as it does at the bottom of the Little Hill with a suitable approach to the Wrekin.

Eaton-upon-Tern 🌿

Eaton-upon-Tern is a small hamlet in the parish of Stoke-on-Tern, approximately half way between Great Bolas and Childs Ercall. Over a hundred years ago Eaton-upon-Tern was a large and flourishing estate, owned by the Heatley family, with a community of around 200. It had a large farm with many farm buildings, a mill, a forge, a chapel, a village shop and about a dozen farm cottages.

At the outbreak of the Second World War, Eaton-upon-Tern suddenly and dramatically became an important air base. The advance party of REME arrived to demolish some farm cottages and convert the rich agricultural land into runways, hangars and reinforced concrete buildings to house over 2,000 Royal Air Force personnel. The RAF station was originally called Childs Ercall, but this led to some confusion as there was already another station in the area at High Ercall, so the name was changed to RAF Peplow. Later the Fleet Air Arm took over and the Station continued to be used for training purposes.

After the war the land was at last returned to the farmers. One of the original runways is used by crop spraying aircraft. Part of the runway system was dug up and the rubble used as hardcore on the Newport bypass. Forty years on, the concrete buildings have become eyesores, scars on the otherwise idyllic landscape. Local farmers use some for storage and the old hangars are used as storage depots by several enterprises.

Today the village is much changed. Local children call it 'the conker village' since the road through is lined with alternating pink and white horse chestnut trees, making an attractive green tunnel.

The chapel, shop and mill have all been converted into attractive houses. The old forge is now a garage and store to a modern bungalow. The village farm is no longer the main source of employment and has been reduced considerably in size, to its present 23 acres.

There are no services to the village apart from electricity. Water is from private boreholes and sewage disposal is by septic tanks. There are some business people living in the village but the majority are retired. Within the past 20 years several modern residences have been built and old cottages modernised. The residents enjoy the peace and try to maintain the community spirit.

Eaton-under-Heywood 🌿

A little village – no, a mere hamlet in the 20th century, nestling under the wooded slopes of Wenlock Edge. The road leads to the church, Old Rectory and Manor Farm but goes no further. Today the area relies on farming as it has for the past eight centuries and more. Domesday Book contains references to Eaton, which was originally part of Tickelvorde.

The church standing on the hillside, with its sloping aisle, is dedicated to St Edith of Wilton, an Anglo-Saxon saint, and as the Manor belonged to Wenlock Priory before and after the Norman Conquest it seems likely that the church was founded in Saxon times.

In earlier times there was great hardship in the area. An increase in pauperism is recorded in the 18th century and a spate of pauper burials are recorded in the church register. Again at the beginning of the 19th century with the Enclosure Act Eaton lost 300 acres of common land, which must have caused untold suffering to the families squatting at Heywood Common. The former Hammond farmhouse at Hatton became the Parish Workhouse and was used until the opening of the Union Workhouse in Church Stretton.

The railway came to Eaton when the branch line between Much Wenlock and Craven Arms was constructed, passing through the centre of the village with a station at Harton. Eaton was in fact less isolated 100 years ago than it is today. At the turn of the century local farmers joined together once a year to hire a train to take their cattle and sheep to Wellington market. In the severe winter of 1946 the railway was Eaton's only link with the outside world. For 6 weeks the milk was hauled by horse and sled across fields via New Hall to Harton where it was put on the train. Essential provisions for the houses had to be hauled in on the empty sled.

A National School was built in 1860 half way between Eaton and Ticklerton to serve both villages. It closed in 1926 when there were only 14 pupils and after a storm had blown down the belfry, sending stones and planking through the schoolroom roof and hurling the bell into the playground. It was then used as a clubroom for the parish.

With the introduction of a large poultry enterprise there is now work for the young women in the village and the roar of tractors and powerful machinery in the fields indicates that though this parish only has 180 souls compared with 546 in 1871, Eaton is still thriving.

Edgmond 🦢

The village of Edgmond, lying close to Newport off the A41, was mentioned in the Domesday Book. Edgmond was then the Manor and Newport a mere appendage.

The focal point is the church and here, on what could have been the site of a previous Saxon one, a beautiful Norman church was built from local sandstone. Many of the Norman features were later replaced by Gothic architecture.

A custom originating in medieval times was revived in Edgmond in 1867, called the Church Clipping, meaning Clasping of the Church. There are only two other churches in England where this still takes place. The clergy, choir and congregation parade to form a circle around the church while singing the hymn *We love the place oh God*. Prayers and the Blessing end the service. Up until 1939 this was followed by the Edgmond Wakes – small fairs used to visit the village and the village Flower Show took place.

Local people are fortunate in being able to purchase produce from the National Poultry Institute shop which is part of the well known Harper Adams Agricultural College. This college occupies over 300 acres and is a great asset to the village providing work, workers' houses, students' quarters and lodgings in local homes.

To quote the Bible 'the lion shall lie down with the lamb', but the Edgmond Lion and Lamb, being inns, stand separated by 600 yards. In addition to the post office, there is a good general shop, hairdressing salon and newsagents, delivering daily papers.

In the last century there was rivalry between the people of Edgmond and Tibberton, a village to the west of Edgmond. This was recorded in a jingle:-

'Tibberton Tawnies,
Cherrington Cats,
Edgmond Bulldogs
and Adeney Cats
Edgmond Bulldogs made up in a pen,
Darna come out for the Tibberton men.'

Edstaston & Coton

Edstaston and Coton are scattered communities situated between Wem and Whitchurch. Coton Hall originally owned the large estate which covered Whixall and Coton itself. This is a very attractive and well-built house, and can be seen across the fields from the Wem-Whitchurch road.

Come down the road towards Wem, and at Quina Brook can be seen the old lime kilns. The Shropshire Union Canal came up to these kilns,

and was in use until the end of the Second World War. During the 1970s
the canals were sold off and have since been filled in. Also at Quina
Brook, adjacent to the lime kilns, the chapel still stands and is kept in
very good repair.

The famous author and playwright George Bernard Shaw made many
visits to Edstaston, especially when his plays were being performed at
Stratford. Shaw's normal wear for the country was a Norfolk jacket,
knee breeches, woollen stockings and heavy shoes. He hated publicity
and was known to be an agnostic, but when visiting Edstaston he always
attended the local church. Many Edstaston people still remember GBS to
this day walking the lanes.

Edstaston church is probably one of the finest gems of its kind still to
be found in this country. It is unique in that although it dates back to
Norman times and still retains its Norman features, it did not attain
parish status until 1850. What is amazing is that its former humble
chapel status does not accord with the richness of the church it is today.
It still has wall paintings, more easily seen today, as they have been
carefully restored.

Like most areas, Edstaston and Coton have seen many changes over
the years. Whereas generation after generation once lived in the same
houses, during the past 15 years this has changed, with many new people
from all over the country moving to this idyllic setting.

Ellerdine

Before the Norman Conquest, Ellerdine was held by Dodo, a free man,
and the manor subsequently passed through many hands. In 1930 the
estate was sold, many tenants buying their own properties.

Ellerdine school, schoolhouse and village hall occupy the corner of a
field that is identified on the old tithe maps by the name of Nightly
Brockles. The money for the present brick built hall, which also incorpo-
rates the old schoolmaster's house was raised over the years by all kinds
of efforts.

The Wesleyan Methodists of Ellerdine scraped together their pennies,
and in 1813 built Emmanuel Chapel. Descendants of members who
signed the Trust Deed still worship there, and at least one holds office. In
1847 the Primitive Methodists staged a breakaway and built Bethel
Chapel at the other end of the lane, adding in 1866 a room to house their

day school. Both chapels are now re-united.

Grandfather clocks were made many years ago at Oakgate Farm, Ellerdine Heath. Nowadays people come from far and wide to 'pick their own' strawberries, beans etc, at the same holding.

Just across the road is the officially named Royal Oak Inn, though no one ever calls it that, always The Tiddlywink. Up to the 1930s the beer was served in what appeared to be the licensee's living room, drawn straight from the barrel into a jug. The packed car parks are evidence of the Inn's present popularity.

The households of Ellerdine and surrounding villages are fortunate in that they can have something that is rather rare delivered on their doorsteps – bottles of Gold Top with a green line across the cap. This means that the rich Jersey milk has not been pasteurised. It is farm bottled, and its only preservative is super clean production and careful handling.

Ellerdine Railway Siding opened in 1930. It had a large weighbridge, and for its custodian, a brick hut with a coal stove.

In 1926–7 14 council houses were built near Ellerdine Council School in pairs, each with a pigsty, and usual offices. One borehole and one pump served them all for water. When in 1954 another 10 homes were erected across the road a brick tower housed a tank, that was kept full by an automatic electric pump, giving piped water to all the houses. Since 1965 the whole district has enjoyed mains water supply.

Farlow

Farlow is a small scattered community with a church, school and post office; a collection of scattered houses and farms linked by narrow, winding lanes. The tiny post office is in the lower part of the village, near the old village centre, by the well. Originally it was a typical crossroads settlement, complete with thatched houses, a blacksmith and a wheelwright for running repairs. The blacksmith's shop is still in existence and was in use until the 1950s. There was a corn mill, now a house, rebuilt in 1805 and working until the 1940s.

Prior to the building of the present church an old chapel was situated at the bottom of Farlow Bank, close to The Bush which was then an inn. One can still see the track of the old road, on which the chapel lay, passing to the lower side of The Bush. The new church was also sited next to an inn, the Maypole Inn (now Hillhead Farm), in the Green Meadow, reputed to have been the venue for cockfighting etc. In 1865 a school was built next to the church. This school, drawing nearly 50 pupils from four villages probably enjoys the best view of any in Shropshire. Driving past the school and down 'the Bank' can be rather frightening. Some locals, even, will drive an extra mile or so out of their way to avoid it, but it is now more than 30 years since the last car plunged over the edge into the Church Meadow below.

Well over a mile from the post office towards the Clee Hill, lies the one remaining village public house, The Gate Hangs Well. Behind this inn, up a maze of rough tracks, can be found yet another part of this scattered village. Hill Houses were the cottages and smallholdings of what was originally a mining community. Lime, iron and coal were all worked in this area from Roman times, and mining was, until the turn of the century, the second largest source of employment. Now residents of the village have a wide variety of employments, but almost the only ones who do not have to travel away to find that work are the farmers.

Fitz

Grafton School was originally the recreation and living quarters for the Air Force servicemen who were stationed on Forton Airfield. The Airfield was built and developed from 1940 and ceased to be operational in 1946. The previous school at Fitz next to the church was overflowing with pupils and some had to have lessons in the village hall. The departure of the Air Force from the Grafton area left an ideal building complete with hall, kitchens and three classrooms. The move from Fitz to Grafton took place in 1950 and in 1963 more pupils joined the school when Montford and Shrawardine village school closed. During recent years the numbers of pupils have declined but there are still 2 teachers and a thriving Mother and Toddler group meeting once a week.

The present church of St Peter & St Paul was built in 1722, replacing an earlier medieval building built in the 12th century. The last baptism took place in the old church on 26th October 1722. In 1972 plans were made and carried out for the landscaping of the churchyard, when many gravestones were moved to the sides of the burial ground to make the maintenance and the grass cutting easier.

Ford 🌿

Sixty years ago, Ford village was small, and the life of the community was centred around the church, the school and the Methodist chapel. The church was known as Ford Chapel in the 12th century. One of the existing two bells dates back to that time. Chavel is part of Ford, and was a garrison against the Welsh, including Owen Glendower.

The Shropshire & Montgomery Railway, also known as the Potts railway line, once travelled through Ford from the station in Abbey Foregate, Shrewsbury, to Llanymynech. There was a station for passengers and a coal yard. Local children called the S & M Railway the Slow & Miserable Railway.

Agriculture was the main industry of the district, so the majority of the work force was devoted to the land. The village shop also had a post office and bakery – and the baker still lives in Ford. Oh, what a lovely smell greeted you on the way home from school! If a loaf was purchased, the crusts were not always intact on arriving home!

Ford had two inns, Cross Gates and Pavement Gates in Chavel, and a blacksmith's shop kept busy by the farmers. Along the road opposite the chapel was a cobbler's shop and a little sweet shop.

Ford also possesses a Roman stile and cruck house in New Street. In Butt Lane, the pool there was a great attraction especially when frozen hard for the village children to slide on.

Ford village remained the same for many years, until after the Second World War. In 1947, Atcham Rural District Council began building the 70 houses on the Leasowes field. Later 16 one-bedroomed flats were built, followed by 18 bungalows for senior citizens, with warden accommodation. As a result of the increased number of children, a new school was built on the then school playing fields.

The village amenities now include:- two hotels, a garage, a playing field. for the village children; a new village hall, street lighting, main sewerage, post office and stores, as well as many active organisations.

Frodesley 🌿

The parish today is one of scattered farms and cottages. The original village settlement lay along the village street, which runs southward at right angles from the famous Roman Watling Street. Industry did once

67

exist in Frodesley and was based on coal seams which underlie the clay to the north and west of the main village. The brickworks to the north of the village produced tiles, bricks and drainage pipes and marl pits are commonly found as ponds. Frodesley had a smithy in 1724 and a carpenter, a cooper, two shoemakers, a shopkeeper and a tailor in 1856. However by 1926 only the village shop, the cobbler and the Swan Inn remained, and both the shop and the cobbler closed soon after 1941.

There has never been a school in Frodesley and the children have always attended Acton Burnell or Longnor schools.

Frodesley church is first recorded in the 13th century. It was originally a chapelry of Condover and burials took place at Condover until Frodesley's own churchyard was consecrated in 1780. The churchyard is home for a splendid example of the rare Monterey Cypress (*Cupressus macrocarpa*) which was introduced from California in 1836. It is a notable tree, having a girth of 1.67 m when measured in 1982.

At the side of Lodge Hill close to Hoar Edge and the Causeway can be found the Frodesley Oak. This has been in a poor state since the turn of the century but still stands and hangs determinedly on to life with a few fresh leaves appearing each year. The girth of the Frodesley Oak was 7.77 m in 1946 and is only slightly more now, because the rate of growth has been virtually zero for many decades.

The village has so far escaped radical development and has thus managed to retain its quaint character. Despite the high efficiency of the farming practiced in the locality, the character of the farming landscape around Frodesley has so far escaped drastic change.

Garmston 🌿

Midway between Leighton and Eaton Constantine, in a peaceful pastoral setting, lies Garmston.

Once just a collection of two farms and a few cottages, Garmston now has many new dwellings. The extensive farm buildings of Garmston House, where once pigs were housed and piglets squeezed under the gates to run free in the lanes, have in recent times been converted into modern dwellings.

Standing in the centre of the village is Yew Tree House, dated 1622. The black and white house, originally thatched now tiled, was once a smallholding and also used as a butcher's shop. Opposite the top of the Rudge are two thatched cottages. Here once lived Mr Jack Needham, a blacksmith, and Mr Percy Hopcroft, a renowned thatcher. Examples of

Mr Hopcroft's craft can be seen at the White House Museum near the Abbey in Shrewsbury.

At the bottom of the Rudge, a very steep road, you come to Leighton at Townsend Cottage. This junction is of interest because of the Cressage turnpike which joined it here and tolls had to be paid. It is also the point where the Leighton and Eaton Constantine road joins to encircle Garmston.

Many cottages have been renovated and modern infilling started in Garmston in 1960 thus altering the character of the hamlet, the occupations of its inhabitants are now mainly industrial and professional.

Gobowen 🐝

Gobowen is situated about 3 miles north of Oswestry on the old A5 road, but now has a new by-pass which takes most of the through traffic. It is very near the Welsh Border and surrounded by lovely countryside.

The older part of the village is clustered around the railway station, which has always been of great importance. It first appeared in the Great Western Railway timetable in 1848. The station building became a listed building when it was discovered that its Italianate style of architecture is quite unique. It is now in the process of being renovated.

Around the central Square, where at one time a fountain stood, is the war memorial and the main shopping centre. There are two public houses – The Cross Foxes and the Hart and Trumpet, a working men's club, two petrol stations, a repair garage, and an excellent library.

Gobowen has 4 places of worship. The Anglican church was built in 1896 and was destroyed by an arson attack on 27th December, 1979. Funds for rebuilding flowed in from many sources and only two years after the fire, the church was re-opened for worship. Preeshenlle United Reformed church was built in 1832 and rebuilt in 1862. Part of the church was used as a school from 1868 until the present County Primary School was built in 1907. There is also a Methodist church and a Roman Catholic church.

The Shropshire Orthopaedic Hospital, founded by Sir Robert Jones and Dame Agnes Hunt on the present site in 1919 and renowned throughout the world, is about one mile from Gobowen, and provides employment for many people. There is also the Derwen Training College for the Disabled on the outskirts of the village. Both Hospital and College do wonderful work.

Great Bolas ❧

Great Bolas, or Bolas Magna, is a small village in north Shropshire, equidistant between Wellington and Newport. It lies between two rivers, the Tern and the Meese. The Meese flows into the Tern just below Bolas Bridge.

In the Middle Ages, Great Bolas belonged to one of the foresters who looked after the Royal Forest of Wrekin. In 1284 Hugh Fitzjohn made Great Bolas the most important village in the area by setting up a gallows and holding a twice-yearly court to try cases of theft and murder.

The population has changed little since the beginning of the 19th century, when it was 207, and is a mixture of old established village families and newcomers. At the time of the 1801 count, virtually everyone worked on the land but today a mere handful do so.

The parish church is dedicated to John the Baptist and was officially opened in 1723. There was, however, a small church in Great Bolas as early as 1306. The massive oak pews in the chancel, though somewhat altered, probably belonged to that church.

At Bolas Heath is Burleigh Villa, a large house with a fascinating history. The house was built in 1789 by a Mr John Jones, who had arrived, by chance, in Great Bolas that year. Mr Jones, who was travelling incognito, was none other than Henry Cecil MP, the heir to the Earl of Exeter. He had fled from an unhappy marriage and found solace in the village of Great Bolas. He became friendly with the Hoggins family and lodged with them until the house he was building, now Burleigh Villa, was completed. He became infatuated with Sarah Hoggins and they were eventually married in Great Bolas Church on 13th April 1790. Three years later, following the death of his uncle, Cecil succeeded to the title. Sarah Hoggins, the farmer's daughter from Great Bolas, became the Countess of Exeter.

The school in Great Bolas was closed in 1981. Records show that there was a school in Great Bolas in 1871. Several family names in the first register are still common in the village today.

Great Hanwood ❧

Great Hanwood is a village some 4 miles south west of Shrewsbury, and derives its name from the woods and coppices which are a feature to the present day.

St Thomas' Church, Great Hanwood

During the 18th century, Cobden Corn Mill was established and operated by water from the Rea Brook and had a life of some 200 years. Mill House exists to this day.

In the 19th century, Hanwood became an industrial village and the population, a mere 6 families in 1086 became about 300.

Hanwood Mill was built pre-1810, possibly as a paper mill, but by 1820 the mill housed a flax, yarn and thread finishing factory. The mill continued to expand and cottages were built to house the work force, which, in 1868 stood at 140.

In due course cotton goods superseded flax goods, but in 1886 the mill owners went bankrupt. The mill was taken over by the Wotherton Barytes and Lead Mining Co., and continued grinding the ore and drumming the powder until the mill closed in 1922. Barytes is used to this day in the manufacture of paint. Coal mined within a 2½ mile radius of the village, also provided employment.

Although a small village, Hanwood boasted 2 railway lines – the Potts line, (later renamed the Shropshire & Montgomery Light Railway) originally envisaged as a holiday route to the Welsh Coast for Pottery workers, and in 1860 the old GWR and LNW Railway Companies

71

joined forces to construct a railway line from Shrewsbury via Hanwood, Welshpool and Newtown to the coast. This railway was extensively used to carry produce from the mills and the mines as well as providing a passenger service.

The parish church of St Thomas the Apostle is, in its present form, a mid-Victorian building. It was enlarged and rebuilt in the 1850s from an earlier building of about 1700.

The village now has a modern school opened in 1969 replacing the old Hanwood school, Cruckmeole school and Lea Cross school. Hanwood Old School is now a bed and breakfast establishment.

Since the beginning of the 1970s when the village was connected to the main sewerage pipeline, new private and council housing estates have been built, increasing the population from 650 to over 1500. It is now a residential village with people commuting to work to all parts of the county and beyond.

Great Ryton 🦢

An unspoilt hamlet with panoramic views. Ryton was so named because rye grew here on the light soil.

Pinfold Cottage was originally a shepherd's cottage and the garden a sheep pound. The ancient roadside hedge has been dated by its plants as 15th century.

Yew trees are a feature of Ryton and Yew Tree Cottages were once Ryton Manor. There are several interesting buildings here, many of them 16th century.

At Little Ryton there is a pretty cottage with cast-iron Coalbrookdale windows. There is an old Methodist chapel, which closed in 1906, and an old smithy, now rebuilt.

At the Old House the Atkis family lived for three centuries and there was said to be a window with Dick Turpin's signature scratched on it!

Greete 🦢

Greete is a small parish 2 miles north west of Tenbury Wells and 6 miles south east from Ludlow. It gets its name from the old English word Greote meaning gravel river or brook. The brook is the boundary between Greete and Burford on the south east side of the parish.

The church dedicated to St James was built in the 13th century. It has been much modernised. The bells are late 17th century – one is inscribed 'Haste Away Make No Delay'. The rarest possession is the two-light timber framed window situated in the north wall, believed to be over 500 years old.

Opposite the church stands Greete Court, formerly a small moated Manor House. Historians claim that the house was once a 3–4 storeyed, one room square, 4 gabled hunting lodge.

Edward Foxe and his son Charles are attributed with having built Greete Court in its present style. It is brick built with some part timber walls and also has lovely twisted chimneys. In part of the chimney stack is a priest hole where at one time it is alleged King Charles took refuge.

The Foxe family sold the estate to Thomas Edwards in 1639. Thomas was created a Baronet in March 1644 by Charles I. King Charles also gave Thomas one of his little memorial rings with his portrait and this is still preserved at Netley.

The old rectory, now a private residence, was built in 1848. It is thought that a former rectory was the Brick House – its garden joins the churchyard and this is a possibility.

Grinshill

The village lies beneath a steep and thickly wooded hill, with a narrow lane through the heart of it. The houses are built in a wide variety of architectural styles. The most impressive house is the Jacobean Stone Grange which overlooks the cricket field and is known locally as the Pest House; it was built as a country refuge in time of plague by Shrewsbury School in 1617.

The village church, dedicated to All Saints, is tucked away up a lane leading to the woods and hill. It was built of local red stone in 1839–40 and has a small tower with a projecting parapet in Italian manner. The screen, pulpit and pew ends were carved by the Misses Wright, sisters of a former vicar, from an oak grown in the parish at the Pinfold.

The village hall near to the church at the foot of the hill was built as a school in 1862. Ten years later, the school at Clive was built and the school at Grinshill became first a Sunday School and then the village hall. Now, after recent renovation and decoration, it is used for village activities and meetings. For a number of years around 1917, Grinshill had a Brass Band.

Overlooking the village is the hill, a wooded sandstone crag 630 feet above sea level, with superb views of much of Shropshire and distant Welsh mountains. Here, in Corbet Wood, is the first Picnic Area designated in Shropshire (1972) which has space for 40 cars. Later, a Nature Trail was inaugurated. Polecats, sparrow-hawks and kestrels have been seen in the woods.

The old quarry, which is 200 feet deep, is largely overgrown. Here men used to risk life and limb hewing caravan-sized blocks of 10–14 tons to be hauled by steam crane to the top. The stone has been used since Roman times to build many famous buildings and, in the 17th century, was shipped across the Atlantic to Virginia. Today's requirements are different and the stone is mainly bought for decorative walling and fireplaces.

Hadley 🌿

The village of Hadley dates back to Saxon times. It is mentioned in the Domesday Book, when it was known as Hatlege.

One famous person to live in Hadley at Hadley Park Hall was John Wilkinson, the celebrated 18th century ironmaster who was regarded by his workers as a folk hero. Local people thought so well of him that rumours spread that his ghost would return on the 7th anniversary of his death and many expected that his ghost would pull the old industries out of a recession. Thousands gathered and waited in vain for him to ride by on his horse.

The villagers were mainly employed in agriculture until the Industrial Revolution, with a few tradesmen such as websters, weavers and spinners. After 1750 the Rag Field (now known as New Hadley) developed, with coal pits and ironstone workings, although there are few records of industry in Hadley until 1804 when John Wilkinson opened the New Hadley Furnaces.

Leegomery Mill was powered by both water and steam and local farmers continued to grind grain there until 1945. Hadley Park Mill was powered by both wind and water, probably making it the only mill of this kind in Shropshire.

At the time of the Industrial Revolution there was a canal which passed through Hadley, with an incline plane at nearby Trench. This was the last to operate in the British Isles, finally closing in 1921, and a lock at Hadley Park was last used in the 1930s.

74

In 1906 the Sankey family from Bilston took over the Castle Works at Hadley. They brought with them about 100 employees to commence production of car bodies and as this increased local men were employed. Joseph Sankeys & Sons, later to become G. K. N. Hadley, were the village's main employers for a number of years, expanding to over 37 acres with over 6000 employees until a rapid decline in recent years.

The only buildings of interest, the manor house and various old industrial sites were demolished in the 1960–70 period after the arrival of Telford New Town, although a mulberry tree from the manor grounds still stands in Hadley opposite new flats which are named Mulberry Court.

Hadnall

The village of Hadnall is a rather long sprawling village, but very pretty when viewed from the top of Hadnall Bank on the busy A49. The only bit of modern planning is a small and very attractive estate of new private houses and nearby, a new school.

A complete moat, the centre of which was the site of Hadnall Hall, is all that is left of the home of the Bannister family. It was once the hiding place of the two small Princes who perished in the Tower. It is believed that the stone from this house was used to restore the church.

The village shop and post office is long-established and was once a first class bakers and general store, scented with ground coffee, hot bread and Chelsea buns.

The church of St Mary Magdalene stands plain for all to see, surrounded by a well kept churchyard near the road. All the lovely carved oak and stained glass windows were given by Mr Frank Bibby, who, as Lord of the Manor, lived at Hardwicke Hall in the parish. He employed many servants, footmen, butlers, chauffeurs, keepers, etc. Sadly the Hall had to be taken down but his relatives still keep the estate going.

The north end of the village is quiet and select now, but it was once the hub of the village. Here within a few yards stood the local sweet shop kept by Mrs Needham, a blacksmith's shop, a wheelwright's shop, large carpenter's shop and the undertakers. A tailor's shop kept by Mr Rowley employed 5 or 6 people – every man in those days had a tailor-made suit and very hard wearing they turned out to be. Farmers in those days, be they fat or thin, tall or short, dressed in their pink for hunting. In those

75

days uniform was the order of the day. Footmen, keepers, chauffeurs all dressed for work.

A once busy mill and a very busy and pretty station have gone, but Hadnall still appeals to a lot of people and often families return here after a few years.

Halford ✦

The ancient form of Halford's name was Hawkeford, the 'ford of hawkers' and suggests that early travellers crossed the river here and 13th century documents do refer to a bridge at Halford.

The accomplishments of modern technology and craftsmanship are evident in Halford's Norman church. A silver plaque commemorates the heating-system fitted in the Festival of Britain Year 1951, and financed largely by the British Electrical Industry. In 1963 the altar and altar rails, fashioned by local craftsmen, were installed, and a local farmer donated the east window, in which appears a representation of his farmhouse and the now dilapidated village water mill.

The family crest of Lady Mary Windsor-Clive may be seen on the wall of the old school, now a private residence, which she had built in 1876, and which served Halford's children for over 50 years. The original oak doors remain, and the school bell still adorns the building; in the garden stands a fine oak tree, planted by the oldest boy pupil and the youngest girl, to commemorate King George V's Coronation.

High above Halford stands the tower called Flounders Folly, built by Benjamin Flounders. His initials and the date 'B.F. 1838' are inscribed on the building. It is said that he built the tower to view his ships in the Bristol Channel, but on finding his view was blocked, he died of disappointment. His tower had become a folly. Fascinating though this story is, it is generally thought that Benjamin Flounders built the tower simply as a boundary mark.

Harmer Hill & Myddle ✦

Harmer Hill situated in Myddle parish was originally a Saxon settlement. In the Domesday Book it was spelled Mulleht – the wood by the junction of the stream.

Myddle Castle was built by Lord Lestrange of Knockin. It fell into ruin under the custodianship of wild Humphrey Kynaston who was outlawed early in the 16th century and only a fragment now remains. Another Kynaston was rector of Myddle church and chaplain to James II. He offered to rebuild the ruinous tower 'as far as his own height' if the parishioners would rebuild the remainder – they refused. In later years it was rebuilt by John Dod for £5 per yard. Nothing remains of the early church, the present building was rebuilt in 1744 incorporating John Dod's tower.

Richard Gough, the celebrated social historian, was born in 1635 at Newton-on-the-Hill in Myddle parish and educated at the village school and nearby Broughton. His old home is still inhabited. Gough started to write his History of Myddle in 1700. Part I gives a unique insight into ordinary people's lives in Stuart times and how the Civil War affected them. Part II is the most admired and more widely known. Taking the church seating plan Gough wrote about every family pew by pew, from the local squire to the very poor with wit and impartiality. He died in 1723 aged 88.

Harmer Hill was then common heathland, used for peat cutting and grazing by the farmers in Newton-on-the-Hill. The mere was drained in 1634, the last remnant survives as Moss Farm.

The parish is agricultural though sadly few work on the land due to modern farming methods. Sam Mayall of Lea Hall was an early pioneer of organic farming in the county, still carried on by his son.

Most of the older buildings in the parish are built of sandstone quarried locally in the parish. Many new houses have recently been built, their occupants commuting to work but preferring to live in a country village.

There are sub-post offices cum village shops in both Harmer Hill and Myddle which serve their communities well – also 3 excellent pubs.

High Ercall 🌿

High Ercall is a rural village about 9 miles from Shrewsbury and 5 from Wellington. It is now included in the new area known as Telford. It became well known in the Second World War when the Air Ministry requisitioned hundreds of acres of farmland in order to develop an air base known as the High Ercall Aerodrome.

Among the old buildings in the village are the Hall, the church, the Mill House, the Toll House, the smithy, the almshouses and the shop, with some of its windows still bricked up to avoid the window tax of

The Arches, High Ercall Hall

long ago. Of these the Mill House, the Toll House and the smithy have been converted into domestic premises.

The Hall was built on the same site as the Manor House by Sir Francis Newport, an officer in King Charles's army. The Hall was later fortified as a garrison when the Civil War took place. It was badly battered when the Royalists there were besieged for a year before they had to give in to Cromwell's army. The four well-preserved arches at the rear of the Hall are part of the original Manor House built by the de Arkles. the family after whom the village is named.

The beautiful Norman church, facing the Hall and opposite the school, goes back to the 11th century. It, too, was badly damaged during the Civil War when the Royalists, besieged at the Hall, used it as a fort. Shot marks can still be seen on the walls.

The Gospel Oak nearby, under which medieval friars held religious meetings 500 years ago, is now the favourite place for the village youth to congregate.

Every year there are two big events: the Flower Show and Fete and the Autumn Fayre. The former is not a money-making effort but a great opportunity to share an afternoon of fun. If a profit is made it goes to charity. The Autumn Fayre is organized to benefit the church.

Highley 🐝

Highley, with a population of over 3,000, is now one of the largest villages in Shropshire. It is situated in the south-east corner of the county, near the Shropshire-Worcestershire border, and was once part of the very extensive Wyre Forest. It is mentioned in the Domesday Book of 1086, where it is recorded as Huglei. It was named after the Lord of the Manor, Rudolf De Huglei.

The oldest building in the village is the church, built about 1140, and added to over the centuries. It is now in need of urgent repairs.

To the east of the village is that lovely river, the Severn, which in earlier times was a very busy waterway. Here, in the area known as 'Stanley', there had been quarries of sandstone and shallow deposits of coal since the Middle Ages. From this area, stone for Worcester Cathedral was carried downstream, and Highley's first pub, the Ship Inn, received its original licence in 1770. It catered in the main for bargees, colliers and quarrymen.

In 1874, The Highley Mining Company started producing good quality coal at its newly built colliery. As the industry flourished, miners were imported from other mining areas, especially Staffordshire. To cater for this influx in the population, many new houses were built, and today the long streets of miners' houses still survive. By 1931, the population had risen to 2,095, a dramatic increase.

The pit closed in 1969, and the character of the village changed. Since that time, very many new houses have been built, and it is now basically a commuter village.

Few villages can boast of a sports complex such as Highley has. In the past, all miners contributed a few coppers a week towards their Welfare Hall and sports field. Over the years, an area of 11 acres has been developed with facilities for football, cricket, bowling, tennis, swimming and recently a splendid Adventure Playground has been built. In 1961 a purpose-built Youth Club was erected within the 'Welfare' grounds.

The village itself has no claim to beauty, but once you have left the heart of the place, with its rather drab shops and long streets of terraced houses you are in an area of unsurpassed loveliness. To the east is the great beauty of the Severn, to the west the Clee Hill with its spectacular and breathtaking sunsets, to the north the delightful old town of Bridgnorth, and southwards is the Wyre Forest with its wonderful walks and fascinating flora and fauna. Now too, the last evidence of the mining industry has gone, as the old colliery site has been reclaimed and landscaped.

Hinstock ⚘

The earliest written record of Hinstock is in the Domesday Book, 1086. The name is given here as Stoche, but in documents of 200 years later, this has become Hinstok or Hynestok. It probably means the 'place of the monks'.

In 1987, Hinstock had a population of about 700 which has not varied greatly since the earliest census in 1801. It is an agricultural parish of 3,266 acres, with at each end a council housing estate built since 1950. There are a number of family farms, mostly producing milk, sugar beet, potatoes and barley. At the north end of the village there is a 7 acre Nature Reserve.

The school dates from 1839. It was originally a Church foundation, but is now a county school. It has about 60 pupils and 3 teachers.

The principal employer of labour is a flourishing mushroom farm. There is a post office and general store, several market gardens and garages, 2 building contractors, and 3 inns. As well as the church, there is a Wesleyan chapel. John Wesley is said to have preached in the village on one of his visits to Shropshire.

There is a men's club room and a fine village hall built by local subscription in 1961 as a memorial to the fallen of the two World Wars.

The completion of the by-pass in 1983 has greatly reduced the amount of traffic travelling though the centre of the village, thus improving the safety and convenience of this scattered village.

Hodnet ⚘

Hodnet has been described as neither a town nor a village. It certainly has some amenities which other villages lack.

Agriculture is an important industry but fewer men are employed on the farms. Small farms have disappeared, land having been taken over by larger farms and the farm houses becoming desirable residences.

The beautiful Hall gardens and the old church are the features for which Hodnet is best known. The Hall is about 100 years old and was built on the site of an older house. The gardens are visited every year by thousands of people. They were created by the late Brigadier A. Heber-Percy and took 30 years to complete. They are particularly beautiful in the spring when the daffodils and azaleas are in bloom. The Heber-Percy family still live at the Hall.

The church is dedicated to St Luke. Interesting items are a good Norman door, good monuments to the Vernons, Hills and Hebers and a small chained library. The tower is a curious octagonal shape. There are three entrances to the churchyard, the lychgate, the wedding steps and the christening gate, where there are no steps, making it easy for the pram containing the child to be christened to be pushed through. Nowadays babies are brought to the church in a car.

Hodnet has connections with National Hunt Racing. Roy Whiston had a successful stable for 40 years until 1986. Records in the church recall the dangers and sadness which surround this sport.

There is a legend that there was a leper colony near Hodnet. It was situated between Hawkstone and the valley of Paradise. The area is known locally as Leapers Hill, this is probably a corruption of Lepers Hill. It is thought that the lepers walked to the church and watched the service through the leper's window.

A new Fire Station was opened in 1986. It is manned by retained firemen – these men carry out a full time occupation but can be called out in an emergency. A new school was also opened by the Duchess of Gloucester in 1986. It is a school of which the district is very proud.

Hookagate 🍂

Hookagate, 3 miles south of Shrewsbury on the Longden–Pulverbatch road, has many links with the neighbouring village of Annscroft. The name is derived from the Anglo-Saxon Hucke-hey-gate indicating an enclosure of oak trees where deer were often driven from the forests of the Stiperstones for the Royal Hunt.

Cherry Tree Cottage, at the entry to Skimhouse Lane, is the last local example of a wattle and daub house in the area and is now being restored. Skimhouse Lane was the site of a soapmaking factory in

Victorian days – the tallow was skimmed off the liquid in the vats to make soap and candles. Allied to this, the area was renowned for the skill of its laundresses.

The first evidence of mining is recorded in 1741 when a Mr Francis Boothby broke into an underground stream near Hanley House adjacent to Hookagate Bridge. Mineral-rich water was pumped from this stream and for 60 years was bottled as Hanley's Spa Water and had a reputation for alleviating many human ailments. Farming land now covers the area.

Hookagate has the school building and 3 pubs and a Methodist chapel, while its near neighbour, Annscroft, has the parish church, the vicarage and the parish hall.

The most important building in Hookagate is the school. Opened in 1864 and closed in 1975, the building is now the Shrewsbury Teachers Centre. Many modern alterations have been made and very good use is being made of an attractive and functional building.

Elderly people living in the village now recall their school days and adolescence with pleasure. Football was a favourite and still dominates the area, Hookagate United playing in the Shrewsbury Sunday League, but the players no longer live locally – they are the sons and grandsons of the earlier team enthusiasts.

Village life was enhanced by a peripatetic trumpeter, and occasional stalls set up by The Royal Oak. Residents remember a china-selling stall and a fishmonger whose stall was regularly raided by a local cat. Ice cream was sold from a horse and cart and in season, a Breton onion man called. Older people affirm that Hookagate was better served with necessary commodities in the early 1900s than it is now.

Hope Bagot 🐿

Hope Bagot lies in a green valley on the western slopes of Titterstone Clee, and derives its name from the old Celtic Hop, meaning valley, and Baggaert, the family who acquired the manor in the 13th century. Farming (mostly stock) is not intensive, so there are wild flowers and wild life in abundance.

The lanes leading into the parish from Knowbury, Clee Hill, Whitton and the Tenbury Road are very narrow, winding and steep, and often very wet due to blocked culverts and the demise of the 'old road man'. Lovely in summer but in winter hazardous due to ice and snow.

The village straggles all over the parish, the greatest concentration of houses being around the church, others dotted down the lanes or farm tracks. The 'big' house, Hope Court, dates from Georgian times and there is also a Georgian vicarage and farmhouse. The black and white house near the church is 16th century. The Pot House on the lane to Whitton was the old brewhouse to the Elizabethan Whitton Court and many of the other houses may be Tudor or earlier in parts.

The population (now about 55 souls) has fluctuated between 50 and a 100 in the 1800s, in the days when small cottages, fine for two, housed families of a dozen or more. Sadly none of the original families remain, although visitors tell of parents and grand-parents who once lived here. Residents are 'comers-in' over the past 40 or so years. Farming is the principal occupation, other people commute to jobs, work at home or are retired or semi-retired.

The tiny Norman church, with its 13th century tower stands above the lane. The ancient yew in the churchyard has a girth of over 23 ft, which suggests it must be about 1,000 years old.

Legend has it that there was once a monastery in the valley above the church where five paths met. There is an unused hollow way leading thence, lined with the stumps of ancient yews and a Monks field. There is no evidence for this other than a record that a 14th century bishop on his annual visit to the Benedictine Monastery at Bromfield was 'benighted' and sought shelter at the monastery at Hope Bagot. On a clear night the sounds of 'their' bells can be heard stealing over the fields.

There is no village centre, no shop, no pub, but there is a fairly active community life and a pleasant village hall shared by Whitton.

Hope Bowdler 🎋

Hope Bowdler village is situated about 2 miles from Church Stretton on the Much Wenlock road. The actual village is just a small hamlet, part of a very scattered parish, which contains 2 or 3 other small hamlets. The village presents a very picturesque sight from whichever way one approaches it, nestling among the hills, the road winding through it.

Hope Bowdler church goes back to the 13th century, the original church being burned down and rebuilt in the 1600s. It seats around 80 people, has a tower with 6 bells and in at least the last 60 years has always had a choir.

The school was built in 1856 catering for some 40 children and attended by pupils from all surrounding districts. It was always regarded as a very good school until it closed in 1948, the children being transferred to Church Stretton.

The village hall was built in the 1920s and given to the parish by the Benson family. It has served as the centre for the parish social life over the years. In the latter years it has been run by a management committee, organising social and fund raising events and has been the centre for many memorable occasions bringing the whole parish together. One in recent years was the Silver Jubilee celebrations in 1977, when the whole population came together to celebrate, with sports, bonfire, lavish eating and general merriment, a day to remember, with an age range from 2 to 92 years.

Although the village has changed very much over recent years with loss of school etc. and people commuting to far away places, residents hope they can still keep some of the community spirit which they have enjoyed in the past.

Hopesay 🌿

Hopesay means valley (Hope) belonging to Picot de Say, one of the marcher Lords given land by the Norman, William, in return for keeping the Welsh at bay. It is a small village of about 60 people. Tucked into a small valley off the main Clun valley, it is surrounded by Burrow Hill, Aston Hill, Hopesay Hill and the Wart. Burrow and the Wart are Iron Age hill forts. Hopesay Hill is now National Trust owned.

The parish church of St Mary is of Norman origin, the most striking feature being the distinctive Norman arched doorway and carved ram's head at the base of this arch. The nave roof, attracting much admiring comment, is probably 15th century and panelled with chestnut. Much alteration and Victorianisation was carried out in the latter 19th century.

Just north of the main village lies a hamlet called The Fish. One of the houses was once an ale house of this name and next to it is a pair of workmen's cottages known as Fish Cottages converted to one house, extended and now called Oakham House.

South of the village is another narrow valley thrusting deeply into Hopesay Hill called Perry Gutter. Here was once a cluster of cottages, a shop and a blacksmith's forge.

On the eastern slope of Hopesay Hill lies a deserted village called Oldfield, now demolished except for a magnificent stone barn converted to a private dwelling.

84

Probably the oldest building after the church is Hopesay Farmhouse which is in the village centre. Constructed partly of stone, a recent removal of stucco revealed a half-timbered elevation on the northern side. This farmhouse and the church and rectory are Grade II listed buildings.

There are several large houses in Hopesay and their generously-planted pleasure gardens, including splendid trees, give the village its beautiful appearance especially as viewed from the hill tops in autumn.

It is interesting to note that, until the late 1960s and early 1970s many of the village cottages, originally built as servants' cottages for the large houses, were still occupied by people born and bred in or near Hopesay. Indeed, in many cases were still inhabited by folk who had been and some still were 'helping out' at the large houses. Nowadays there is nobody living in the village, house or cottage, of native origin.

Hopton Cangeford 🐌

Hopton Cangeford, or Hopton-in-the-Hole, is a tiny village situated 4½ miles north-east of Ludlow and bordered by the parishes of Stanton Lacy, Clee St Margaret and Diddlebury.

The church was made redundant in 1983. The original church was burnt down and the present one is built of red brick with a small western tower containing 3 bells. There is also a rare crypt belonging to the Rouse-Boughton family, which was sealed off before the sale of the church. Now the building is used for making pottery. The new owners have planted bulbs in the churchyard, and villagers cut the grass to keep it all tidy.

There is a School House, just a small cottage, but there is no history of any school in Hopton Cangeford.

The Old Vicarage has been renamed The Gables. There are three farms near to the village, Little Wood, Upper Wood and Lower Wood. The latter has a Mill Meadow and a Mill Barn but no one remembers a mill. Lower Wood has a sheep-dipping hole consisting of a large pool and a flat stone.

The sole owner of Hopton Cangeford is Miss Mary Rouse-Boughton.

There is no village hall, the small community enjoy their social life mainly at Stoke St Milborough.

Hopton Castle 🐚

Hopton Castle village lies 2½ miles south of the B4368 road between Craven Arms and Clun, situated in a valley surrounded by small hills. It is famous for its 12th century keep, which gives the village its name, as, during the Middle Ages, it belonged to the De Hopton family.

The ruined keep stands on a man-made mound, and originally there was a motte and bailey fortification on the site. During the Civil War, the owner of the castle was Robert Wallop, a Parliamentarian. In 1644 they withstood a siege by a Royalist army of much greater numbers for about 3 weeks, refusing to surrender on several occasions. Finally, after the walls had been damaged by artillery and undermined, they agreed to surrender on quarter for their lives. However, only the Governor was taken prisoner to Ludlow Castle, the rest of the men being brutally killed. The term 'Hopton quarter' became a by-word for savage treachery.

The original church, St Mary's, was probably built about 980, but this was destroyed by fire. The church was rebuilt in 1870, at a cost of £1,000, and Miss Rodney of Park Cottage paid for the entire refurnishings. The name was changed to St Edwards in 1927, when the parish was combined with that of Bedstone, to avoid confusion, as Bedstone's church was also dedicated to St Mary.

The population today numbers 44, and the majority of people are employed in agriculture, forestry and associated industries.

There are 15 houses and one bungalow in the village. The Old Rectory is a very large black and white house with stables and large gardens and lawns. The oldest part of the house is Elizabethan, and above the kitchen are two secret rooms, the leaded windows of which can be seen from outside.

Hopton Castle is a well-kept village of pleasant aspect. It is situated in a beautiful rural area of South Shropshire.

Ightfield 🐚

The village of Ightfield differs somewhat from its near neighbour Calverhall. Both have their own church and are still agricultural communities in the main, but there the similarities end. Ightfield still has a post office and village store, unlike Calverhall, but has no sports facilities other than a small play area for the children and has no village hall or public house.

The rector now has 3 parishes in his charge, Ightfield, Calverhall and Ash, and lives in a new rectory built next to the church of St John the Baptist in Ightfield. Due to the differences between the two villages they have become very closely knit and have many combined clubs.

Ightfield Hall is now a farmhouse and additions were made in 1579. It is said that the avenue of trees, from the Hall to the church, was planted by a knight, William Mainwaring, and the Devil. History has it that they had a wager one night, each planting one side of the avenue, but the Devil lost. He promised that he would win in the end when Mainwaring was buried either inside or outside the church. Mainwaring's tomb was placed under the wall of the church, half inside and half outside! It is said that his ghost still visits Ightfield Hall, driving up in a coach and four with a great bustle and clatter. There are two famous brasses in the church dedicated to William Mainwaring and his daughter.

The village shop used to be a public house called The Lamb Inn. There were several inns in the locality which were probably used as stops for waggoners changing horses between Newport and Chester.

Ightfield school and schoolhouse were built in 1884. Before this there was a school, believed to be a dame school, at the back of the Lamb Inn.

Kemberton 🌿

Kemberton – Chenbritone – is recorded in the Domesday Book. From this early settlement to farming community, then to blast-furnaces, nailmaking and coalmining, then to a residential village. The change has been great.

Kemberton Colliery was owned, together with the nearby Halesfield Colliery, by the Madeley Wood Company. On 4th December 1910 a disaster occurred, when the cage cables snapped, killing men and boy miners. When the mine eventually closed in 1967 it was employing 317 men but at its peak in 1957 it produced 228,974 tons of coal and employed 769.

The church of St John the Baptist and St Andrew, is the 6th on the site. The present one was designed by Joseph Farmer, and built in 1882, with stone from Cosford. During this rebuilding, medieval tiles were found which were copied by the Jackfield factory and laid in the new church.

The churchyard holds the unmarked grave of septuagenarian William Billingsley (Beeley), who died in 1828. At the time of his death, he worked alongside his son-in-law Samuel Walker for John Rose at Coalport China Works. He never disclosed the secrets of his kiln construction, but it is thought that the recipe of his paste for the transparent, superior porcelain he produced was 'discovered' from him by John Randall.

The village school closed in July 1964 with only 16 pupils. It had started life when the land was given by W. H. Slaney of Hatton Hall in 1857.

After the Second World War the village started to undergo its biggest change. Where the blacksmith's, wheelwright's, slaughterhouse, tailor's shops all stood are now the carefully restored houses of businessmen of all degrees, commuting daily to nearby towns and cities.

Kinlet 🌿

Kinlet is a sprawling village of some 400 inhabitants, once mainly employed in agriculture and forestry. The village also had its own mine in the later 19th century. Now largely a commuter village, Kinlet has nevertheless kept its village character of church, school, post office and local hostelry!

The church of St John the Baptist is 13th century and has altered little in outward appearance. It stands slightly aloof from the village on a knoll overlooking Kinlet Park.

The village inn, the Eagle and Serpent, takes its name from the coat of arms of the Childe family, the local squires. It was probably run in conjunction with a smallholding at one time, as there was a huge dairy where butter was churned, as well as a cellar for beer and cider.

There are many interesting buildings in the village but in modern times the most important is probably the village hall, scene of many functions throughout the year. An event of local importance, too, is the annual Kinlet Show, which includes sheepdog trials and horsejumping.

Kinnerley 🌿

Stand where the old pound was and you will get a fair idea of the village. Look across at the church, its red sandstone tower with its magnificent gargoyles and resident pigeons dominating the Square; look left at the Cross Keys Inn, where such a house must surely have existed almost as long as the church, the keys of St Peter symbolising not only worship but hospitality for travellers; look right at the shop and post office, another centre where goods and gossip are sold and bartered!

Over Kinnerley bridge lie Lady Ida's Cottages, named after the well on the opposite side – the sulphurous waters were sold in specially named ewers. Lady Ida is portrayed at Weston Hall, a beautiful former Lady Bradford.

Eastwards, the road passes through the hamlet of Dovaston, with its Royal Oak Inn, up the bank past the United Reformed Church to Knockin Heath and onwards to the A5.

Southwards, the road leads to the river past the new school and the evocatively named hamlets of Turfmoor and Edgerley. On this road too, is a monument of the past: Belan Bank, the emasculated but persistent remains of a motte and bailey castle built by the Normans, the scene of 200 years of Welsh–English conflict.

Gone are the days of the Shropshire & Montgomeryshire, or Potts, railway, with such engines as Pyramus, Hesperus, Thisbe, Daphne and Dido. Gazelle, nicknamed the Coffee Pot, is in York Railway Museum and the Queen Victoria Coach, upholstered in royal blue, is a relic of glorious days on the south coast. Those were days, not only of travel to towns but of outings across the rickety Melverley Bridge to Criggion and thence to Breidden.

And so return to Kinnerley Square, where the church stands, a witness of so much of the past and a monitor of today. Outside is a medieval cross, once used for teaching and now surmounted by a sundial given by churchwardens in 1828. This church has continued from early Saxon beginnings, through alterations over the centuries.

Knockin

Knockin is a pleasant and interesting village of less than 200 inhabitants situated 5 miles southeast of Oswestry and 11 miles northwest of Shrewsbury. The name Knockin is said to be derived from an old Welsh word meaning Red Bank. Its history dates back to the 12th century when a castle was sited in the village, one of many along the English–Welsh border.

The church stands near the centre of the village and is surrounded by a churchyard with a lychgate. Only one wall of the original church remains. A priest's doorway can still be seen on the outside of the chancel. Through this, the priest used to enter from the castle side. The graveyard was consecrated in 1871, before this all burials took place at Kinnerley.

The Avenue, Knockin

The Earl of Bradford originally owned most of the lands in and around the village. Many former inhabitants were employed on the Bradford estate, other main industries being malting and farming. These days most people go out of the village to their work.

Today there is a small council estate in Church Lane with some family houses and flats and bungalows for elderly people.

A modern site of interest is the Radio Telescope, one of several across the country linked up with Jodrell Bank. Another unusual feature is the village clock. Many travellers will have seen it on the front of the Bradford Arms. It was placed there in 1902 so that it could easily be seen, if it had been put on the church, it would have been out of view for most people.

Knowbury 🐝

The village of Knowbury is unusual inasmuch as it came into existence as recently as 1840, formed from the parishes of Bitterley and Caynham. Even today it is still only an ecclesiastical parish, with administration of rates etc. in the original civil parishes. The name Knowbury is reputed to stem from Knwe, literally meaning a bump, and bury which is a centuries old name for a collection of dwellings.

In the late 17th century iron ore was mined in Knowbury and transported to Bringewood where it was smelted in charcoal furnaces. Later local furnaces were established and at the beginning of the 19th century there existed an important and sophisticated ironworks.

Coal mining and limestone quarrying provided other employment for a growing population. The roadstone quarries on Clee Hill were developed somewhat later. Families came here from the Black Country and Wales. With so much industry, 'squatting' flourished and a large number of these cottages and smallholdings are still owned by descendants of the original owners. In principle a man could erect a dwelling between the hours of sunrise and sunset, one condition being that smoke be visible. Most of those in existence today still have the characteristic large chimneys.

There are few really old buildings. The old post office at the crossroads has been in the occupation of the Genner family for over 300 years. The Old Farm on Snitton Lane dates back to the early 17th Century with the original timbers visible. Originally it lay on the old drovers road and served as an inn to passing travellers. Later it was to play host to a tile works and clay pits.

The Anglican church was consecrated on 29th January 1840 by the Bishop of Hereford. The present vicar is in charge of 5 parishes.

The centre of the community has always been around the local public house and the shop. The Crown public house was sold in 1968 and is now a private house. The post office cum general stores is very busy and is a good place for meeting friends and exchanging news. After the Second World War a committee was formed with the intention of building a Memorial Hall to be a focal point for recreational interests. Previously all group activities had taken place in neighbouring parishes. Many families gave regular subscriptions and volunteered their services to raise the amount needed. The Memorial Hall was opened in 1960.

Kynnersley 🌿

The village of Kynnersley is situated approximately 13 miles northeast of Shrewsbury and is part of the triangle of land between Wellington, Newport and Crudgington. This area, known as the Weald Moors or 'Wild Moors' was originally low and boggy, with a few settlements on areas of higher ground. These were known as eys or islands, hence the name Kynnersley from Kinardus island – Kinardeseye.

The parish church of Kynnersley is dedicated to St Chad and is a 12th century foundation. The church seats 140 people and is distinguished by a minstrel gallery at the west end, where the two-manual organ is situated.

The oldest remaining house is Whym Cottage, built in 1559 and occupying the centre of the village, opposite the church. Originally built of wattle and daub, the roof remained thatched until the early part of this century. Although some alterations have been made, it is still essentially a 16th century house and is now a Grade 1 listed building. The manor house, also in the centre of the village, has a room known as the Court room, which was used until about 1840. Local tradition is that inhabitants convicted of crimes by the court were hanged from the tree on the Whym – a raised triangular mound in the middle of the village, and then buried in the orchard of nearby Whym Cottage or on the Whym itself.

For most of its early history Kynnersley was surrounded by water especially during the winter months. Funerals conducted at Kynnersley were forced to take the body to Edgmond for burial. Cattle left to graze on common ground on the Weald Moors were equipped with a bell around the neck so that they could be traced if they wandered too far for safety. However, by the beginning of the 19th century, almost all the land had been enclosed by the Duke of Sutherland.

By the middle of the 20th century, great changes had taken place in the pattern of village life, particularly in employment. The closure of the post office, the shop and in particular the village school in 1965, together with government rural transport policy, had a disastrous effect on village life.

Today the village is facing further changes. The development of the new town of Telford, although bringing problems to the area, has also brought many benefits. A well-developed motorway system is accessible within two miles of the village, together with an extensive shopping centre. A new hospital to serve the whole of the Telford area is being built about 4 miles away.

Lawley ✿

The village of Lawley dates back to Domesday times and has remained a tightly knit community until the present day.

The open cast mines which provided the main source of employment for Lawley men for centuries were gradually closed down after the Second World War along with many iron foundries in the neighbourhood. This caused a great deal of unemployment in the village which even the advent of the Telford New Town has done little to alleviate. There is, however, a thriving shop, school and church in the village.

Earlier in this century some of the church festivals had their own local pagan versions in the village. On Shrove Tuesday for instance the children could go 'soling' and knock on doors to beg a pancake or one of the ingredients needed to make it. Then on Good Friday it was customary to nail a hot cross bun to the rafters in order to keep bad luck away from the house in the coming year. But the real favourite of the season was the 'Eaving Days'. These took place on Easter Monday and Tuesday, when any boy was at liberty to grab a girl who took his fancy and 'heave' her up off her feet, without asking permission – it is said a good time was had by all!

Adjoining Lawley until recently was the small hamlet of Newdale, purpose-built by the Darbys of Coalbrookdale as England's first new town in 1759. It contained the earliest example of back-to-back housing in the country and possibly the world, which though not something most people would be proud of now, represented a great improvement on the standard of housing for industrial workers at the time. There was a furnace, a foundry and a forge to employ the people and a Quaker meeting house to cater for their religious needs. For reasons which are not yet clear this enterprise failed and for 200 years the hamlet survived as housing for miners and even as storage for explosives for use in the mines.

New Dale Farm, Lawley: formerly 18th century ironworking buildings

Eventually in the 1960s most of the hamlet of Newdale was condemned and demolished as a slum. By a strange twist of fate in 1987 the Telford New Town Development Corporation suddenly threatened to obliterate all remains of Newdale for ever by permitting open cast mining. A six week archaeological rescue dig was mounted and able to reveal this unique site just ahead of the picks and shovels.

Lea Cross ✿

The hamlets of Lea Cross, Cruckton, Cruckmeole, Arscott and Plealey lie some 5 miles from Shrewsbury and less than 15 miles from the Welsh border in the valley of the Rea Brook.

Lea Cross itself is so named because it lies at the crossroads of the A488 Shrewsbury–Bishop's Castle road, and the minor road from the hamlet of Lea to that of Arscott. It boasts a church, shop cum post office and public house, the only hamlet of the five to possess such amenities.

The church was built out of spite in 1888 when the Reverend Hawkes quarrelled with the Rector of Pontesbury. The dedication to St Anne is in memory of his daughter and the church has never been consecrated. Only recently have baptism and funeral services been allowed, but weddings are still not permitted and interments have never taken place.

Cruckton and Cruckmeole are hamlets which have decreased in size since their heyday in the 19th century. Both take their names from the Celtic Crug meaning hill, so that Cruckton is the settlement on the hill.

Cruckton's greatest claim to fame in the farming world is the annual Ploughing Match to which it gave its name, and to which competitors come from all over Britain.

The Old Hall, Cruckmeole, built by William Philips in the year of the Armada 1588 is a lovely black and white timber frame house. After falling into disrepair for many years it has been renovated and restored to its former glory. Cruckmeole once boasted three corn mills but only one remains and this is now a private residence. The only school in the area is near Cruckmeole, opened in 1969.

Like Cruckton and Cruckmeole both Arscott and Plealey are mere shadows of their former selves. The name Arscott is again from Anglo-Saxon times, the Cott belonging to Aepelred, while Plealey dates from the early medieval period and comes from play – glade: the forest clearing where young deer played.

Lying as it does on the Shrewsbury coalfield there are several old mineshafts in the area, not so long ago an open hazard but now made safe. Few of the miners now survive as the last mine was closed in the Second World War, but during the 19th century there was much activity. At one time there was a flourishing brickworks at Cruckmeole. The bricks were fired by coal from Hanwood Colliery and Hanwood Bricks became well known. Scoring caused by coal wagons is still evident on the road bridge over the Cambrian Coast Railway.

Today farming is the major local industry. Few new houses have been built since the Second World War. Many of these and other renovated older houses are occupied by commuters who work in Shrewsbury, Telford and further afield.

Leebotwood 🍃

Leebotwood is situated on the A49 between Shrewsbury and Ludlow. In the 1930s the road was more like a country lane, with very little traffic.

The Pound Inn, Leebotwood

Most of the land in the village had been made into smallholdings by Shropshire County Council, and the Milk Marketing Board were just beginning to market milk so that most of the holdings would send one or two 10-gallon churns every day, the cows having been milked by hand. The farmers hatched their own eggs in small incubators and the eggs would be sold to the local packing stations.

The railway station was a hive of activity, employing one important station master, two assistants, and the signal box had about four men attached to it. There was a coal wharf run by the Evason family and the local farmers would come by cart to collect feed and any stock they had bought at market.

The church is a wonderful little stone building up on a hill to the west of the village. Supposedly the light from the tower window was to guide travellers across the Long Mynd.

Very little building was done for years, but recently 6 bungalows and 8 houses have been built by Shrewsbury and Atcham Council. The smallholdings have been made bigger for present day farming needs.

Lee Brockhurst 🌿

Lee Brockhurst snuggles peacefully at the foot of the wooded slopes of Lee Hill. Called Lege in the Domesday Book (1086), a clearing or piece of open land, by 1272 it had become Lege-Subtus-Brockhurst, literally 'a piece of open land under a badger hill'.

The village was of strategic importance on the main road between Shrewsbury and Whitchurch with an ancient bridge over the river Roden. The present sandstone bridge was built in 1800 to Telford's design and leads to the village green, overlooked by the North Shropshire Hunt kennels, and by what was once The Raven Inn. Beyond the river on the east lie the old forge, school and shoemaker/wheelwright shop.

Foxhunting began around here in the late 18th century. The first meet was in 1778. Twenty five years later the Lee Bridge Subscription Pack of foxhounds was formed and its first huntsman was John Taylor in 1805. These kennels were not in continuous use until the 1830s when Sir Rowland Hill became master.

The road winds upwards through red sandstone towards the old centre of the village passing the old pound and the oldest house – 15th century. Two more timber-framed houses, 16th century, sit one on each side of the tiny 12th century sandstone church. In fact, 6 houses are listed as of outstanding historic interest, sadly no longer thatched. Nearby was an old village shop, and ancient burial ground.

The population has varied surprisingly little over the years, reaching a peak of 165 in 1841, now around 120. A few new houses have been built on the periphery of the village but as families are smaller the population has declined.

Leighton 🌿

The village of Leighton is bounded on the south by the river Severn and on the north by the Wrekin and is of great antiquity. It has been said to be the most beautifully situated village in Shropshire, lying as it does along the slopes of a deep valley.

Leighton Hall stands on an impressive site on the side of the river with panoramic views of Wenlock Edge and the Stretton Hills. In the grounds stands Leighton Lodge, birthplace of Mary Webb, Shropshire's famous authoress and poet.

The parish church of St Mary the Virgin lies hidden from the road by a thickly wooded drive to Leighton Hall. It was rebuilt in 1716 on the site of a Norman church and has many items of great interest.

The village inn is the Kynnersley Arms, with a mill attached at the rear, the old mill wheel can still be seen. It was once a furnace where cannon balls were cast for the Civil War.

Until the Industrial Revolution the occupations of the Leighton inhabitants were pastoral and revolved round the 'Big House', the church, the school and the larger farms. Then Abraham Darby, the ironmaster, used the furnaces at Leighton and traffic began to come up the river from Bristol to Welshpool in large sailing barges and trows.

The turnpike was opened to coach and horses, farm vehicles, and carriers from Shrewsbury to Ironbridge. A new road was cut through producing Leighton Bank. Life which had altered slowly since medieval times was caught up in the industrial race against time to deliver manufactured goods from Coalbrookdale and the Severn Gorge.

In 1862 the Severn Valley Railway was opened and horse drawn traffic slowly died out to be replaced by motorised traffic and transport. The character of the village has slowly changed from rural simplicity, to adapt to present times.

Lilleshall 🐑

Lilleshall lies on the north east boundary of Telford and has a population of just over 1000. It is dominated by the Hill (known in Saxon times as Lilla's Hill). The imposing monument on the top was erected to the memory of the first Duke of Sutherland by his tenants in 1839. There are extensive views from the Hill over the Shropshire Plain to the Clee Hills, the Wrekin, Haughmond Hill and the Breiddens.

On the south side of the Hill stands a 13th century church of St Michael and All Angels, built on the site of a Saxon church. The tower was added in the 15th century and the church was enlarged in the 17th century to accommodate the increasing population.

Not far from the ruins of an Augustinian Abbey, amongst the woods, stands the imposing Hall of the Dukes of Sutherland. It has beautiful gardens and a ballustraded terrace. Today the Hall belongs to the Central Council for Physical Recreation and many famous sports persons enjoy the facilities provided.

At the west end of the village is the Old Hall, built on the site of an

98

Lilleshall Hill

earlier structure, which in some way was connected with the Abbey. The pool at the Old Hall was originally a monk's pool and the depth was increased during the 1800s. Today it is fished by a village syndicate.

Until the Industrial Revolution, Lilleshall was mainly a farming community and there are several 16th century houses and barns remaining today. During the Industrial Revolution, Lilleshall became an important mining area, with the exploitation of valuable limestone deposits to feed the expanding iron-smelting industry at Coalbrookdale. The limestone workings date back to the latter part of the 17th century and ceased in the late 19th century, after the disastrous flooding of the Church Aston workings. The flooded quarries and their surrounding woodlands off Barrack Lane are very attractive today.

Linley

Linley is a small village attached to Willey and Barrow. It is a very rural and scattered village which stretches from the Broseley-Bridgnorth road on the west side to the river Severn on the east. In the days of steam trains

Linley boasted a very orderly station which often won the prize for the best kept on the Severn Valley Line.

The church at Linley dates back to the 12th century and is dedicated to Saint Leonard. It is a tiny but very beautiful church which stands alone in Linley Drive. The name Linley is Anglo-Saxon and means a clearing where flax grows. On a blocked up doorway on the north side of the church etched into the stone work is a very strange looking creature sometimes known as 'The Little Green Man'.

Linley Hall, not far away from the church is an Elizabethan mansion now converted into flats. Another interesting house is the Hem Farm, an old Jacobean black and white dwelling.

Linley today is still one of Shropshire's most beautiful little villages unspoilt by the passage of time, with lovely leafy lanes and edged by quiet waterways. Together with Willey and Barrow Linley makes up the very large estate known as Willey Estates, owned and farmed by Lord Forester.

Little Wenlock

At 700 feet above sea level, Little Wenlock is one of the highest villages in Shropshire. It is perched at the side of the Wrekin and can only be approached by one of the four steep hills, which means that in severe winters the village often gets cut off. Its height brings special weather conditions, usually mistier and windier than those of its lower lying neighbours, but a fine day more than compensates by offering breathtaking views of the Wrekin, Wenlock Edge, the Severn Valley and the Stretton and Clee Hills.

For most of its existence Little Wenlock has been dependent on opencast mining for its livelihood. So important was the coalfield at the beginning of the 18th century that Abraham Darby laid wooden rails and transported the coal in carts with cast iron wheels, down to the foundry at Coalbrookdale. This 'ginny rail', as it was known locally, is believed to be one of the earliest railways in existence. Mining no longer plays a significant part in the village economy; there is, however, still enough coal in some people's gardens for them to dig it up and fuel their own fires! One other legacy is a recently installed plant to wash opencast coal for use in industry, which is situated just outside the village in an area called Coalmoor.

Earlier this century there were five working farms in the centre of the village, some of which made cheeses to sell at the local market. Of these farms only one now survives, the others having been sold, their land split up, in some instances built on, and their farmhouses converted to ordinary dwellings. Within the last 30 years the village school has fallen victim to the modern trend to smaller families, and village children are now collected by bus – or landrover in the winter – to be transported to Dawley 4 miles for their education. The parish church of St Lawrence, a red brick Victorian building on an earlier site, no longer possesses its own rector, but shares a ministry with the parishes of Ironbridge and Coalbrookdale. Although the old rectory and school, along with the parish rooms and workhouse have ceased to fulfil their original functions, the buildings have survived as private houses.

In the 1930s it was felt that Little Wenlock lacked a focal point for its social life and so a village hall fund was started with £4, the profit from a whist drive held in the school. Through hard work and determination the villagers raised enough money to build a village hall.

Llanyblodwel 🐚

Six miles from Oswestry, in the beautiful Tanat Valley, is the hamlet of Llanyblodwel. There are various versions of the name. In the Domesday record it is given as Bodowanham.

Llanyblodwel was in the principality of Wales until 1573. In AD200 it was a Druid settlement, and it is said that the present church is built upon the Druid circle. Many battles were fought during the period of the Roman occupation. The hill nearby was rich in copper, zinc and lead and the Romans defended these mines. The church of St Michael the Archangel is 1,700 years old, and is one of the oldest holy sites in Britain.

The Pack Horse bridge over the River Tanat was erected in 1710. The record of a bridge on this site goes back as far as 1684. Over the bridge is the black and white 15th century coaching inn, the Horse Shoe, dated 1445. The mounting block still remains. There was a blacksmith's shop under the spreading chestnut tree – still there. Whilst the horses were being shod, the men would go into the Horse Shoe for home baked bread, cheese and pickles, and home brewed real ale.

The beautiful lychgate at Llanyblodwel was erected by the family in memory of William Henry Perry Leslie of BrynTanat, who died on Whit Sunday 1926, aged 66 years. He was a well known musician in his day and was asked by the N.F.W.I. to choose a suitable anthem for the

Women's Institute. *Jerusalem* was his choice. He is buried in the churchyard.

Chief employment is farming and quarrying, the granite from Blodwel quarries is used mainly for road works. Years ago the young folk leaving school went into local employment, now they favour town employment.

A Rhydmeredudd Bridge (Meredudd's Ford) over the River Tanat is supposed to be haunted. On a field on the bank of the Tanat, a gibbet pole was erected to hang those who stole sheep. The apparition has been seen to walk over the bridge at midnight!

Longdon-upon-Tern 🌿

Most of the motorists rushing along the twisting road through the straggling village of Longdon-on-Tern notice the much modernized Tayleur Arms public house. Few see that the dangerous hump-backed bridge over the river Tern is an attractive, single span sandstone arch dating from the 18th century.

A second hump-backed bridge was demolished in 1967 following the abandonment of the Shrewsbury arm of the Shropshire Union Canal. Local farmers reclaimed the land leaving a most important relic of the Industrial Revolution in isolation in a field. It was the first cast iron aqueduct of significant length in the world. It was built by Thomas Telford about 1795.

Hidden behind the Hall, which is a fragment of a Tudor mansion, at the top of Long Bank is the small red brick church of St Bartholomew, built in 1742 and restored by the Victorians.

In the past 20 years many of the old houses have been enlarged and improved and new houses and bungalows built. Since the closing of the railway line and halt, the school, the shop and post office and the petrol station the village is in danger of losing its sense of community.

Longnor 🌿

The village of Longnor, of around 400 inhabitants, lies 8 miles south of Shrewsbury. The name comes from Longenalla – the long alder, which trees line the Cound Brook which runs through the centre of the parish.

Across the A49 from the Longnor turn is The Roundabout, once

102

known as The Bowling Green Inn, a calling place for horse-drawn coaches. Nearby was the smithy (now closed) and an adjacent cockpit, probably frequented by patrons of the inn.

Longnor Hall, built 1670–1694 by the Corbett family, lies in a well wooded deer park, the herd having been established for 700 years. The attractive Carolean house has many interesting treasures.

The old school, built in 1871, which held about 90 pupils in two rooms, is now occupied by Calvert Regan – a real craftsman, turning out beautiful furniture and repairing treasured pieces. Just beyond is the village hall, with large car park shared with the church, worked for 10 years and, aided by grants, built in 1965 and used widely.

St Mary's church, built 1260–1277 has oak box pews made by Richard Lee in 1723. The church is virtually unaltered since its building.

The post office and shop, built about 20 years ago is a great help to many. Opposite is the new school, for about 70 children, with headmaster and 2 teachers. Children are brought by bus and car from adjoining villages and there is a very active Parent Teachers Association.

The Vineyard, a small Council estate built since 1945, has family homes and flats for elderly people. Many well-kept gardens are to be seen in the semi-circle of houses. The Police House, at one end, is now a private dwelling since the loss of the resident policeman, so very much missed.

Many of the old houses are timber framed, later cased in brick, and many have been restored. The Moat House is the oldest house in the village – over 600 years old.

Loppington

Loppington is a typical small Shropshire village, situated about 4 miles west of Wem, and with a population of 250 people.

The church of St Michaels and All Angels, was built in the 14th century quite possibly on the site of a Saxon Church. Loppitone is the old Saxon name for Loppington. The headman of the early settlement was Loppa.

Two of the oldest houses are 16th century, The Nook and Church Farm, in the lane near the church. Not far away the Blacksmith's Arms has an old anvil standing outside as a reminder of its ancient trade.

Loppington has always been a farming community, and the old tan-pit in the village where the hides were treated before being finished, is now the village pond, restored at the time of the Queen's Jubilee in 1977.

Loppington House is of Victorian structure, and the largest house in the village. It was the residence of the Dickin family, principal landowners. Loppington House is now a home for disabled children.

The Dickin Arms, an old ale house recently modernised, does have a claim to fame. In the road outside is the only Bull Ring left in the county. This cruel sport was ended by law in 1835. There is evidence of bear baiting and dancing bears in the village which possibly gave rise to a dramatic incident on the site called Elkes Fallow, opposite the Blacksmith's Arms.

Entrenched in folklore, and originating in the 1880s, it appears that a certain Andrew Wycherley 'Cobbler' going out one misty morning to milk his cow 'spied a Bar'. The alarm was raised and the whole village turned out, Kynaston the miller, and Joseph Harper the shoemaker, with ropes, staves, and dogs, and surrounded with much bravery this evil bear, which turned out in the early light of dawn to be a chump of wood! This epic was put to verse in 1879 and the poem is hanging in the Blacksmith's Arms.

Lydbury North

Lydbury North is a small compact village mentioned in Domesday Book, situated in the south west highlands of Shropshire close to the Welsh Border. It has a fine old church mostly 12th century with a massive 13th century tower. In the south transept is the Walcot Chapel and in the north transept is the Roman Catholic Plowden Chapel. There are very few Anglican churches with a Roman Catholic chapel under the same roof.

At one end of the village lies Walcot Hall, a Georgian house commissioned by Lord Clive of India who lived there after having bought the estate from the Walcot family. His descendants who inherited the earldom of Powis remained at Walcot Hall until 1933 when they moved to Powis Castle and the estate was sold.

Walcot Park has two large lakes and these are inhabited by numerous water and wading birds. There are Canada Geese all the year round but in late summer vast skeins fly in for a long stay.

At the other end of the village lies Plowden Hall the home of the

Walcot Pond, Lydbury North

Plowden family who have lived there since before the crusades. They are the major landowners in the area.

Agriculture has always been the major employment of the local inhabitants. Years ago practically everybody worked on the land but today with modern farming methods far fewer people are required so many have obtained employment in Bishops Castle at the clothing factory and the timber yard.

Years ago there were many craftsmen in the village. A carpenter who was also an undertaker, a blacksmith, a wheelwright and a cobbler who made shoes as well as repairing them, as well as making clogs from local-grown alder wood.

There has been a Church of England school in the village for over 300 years, originally started by a steward of the Walcot family. The first school was held in a room in the church over the Walcot Chapel and can still be seen. The present school was built in the early 1840s but it has been considerably altered and enlarged since that time.

During the last ten years a number of private and estate houses have been built enabling several young families as well as retired people to move in to the village.

Lydham 🌿

Lydham is one of the few border parishes which are partly in England (Shropshire) and partly in Wales (Powys)

Lydham parish is situated between the slopes of Heathmynd ('The Bent') in the north and Aston Hill to the south, between the West Onny and the valley of the Camlad, the only river to flow from England into Wales. The area is of interest to walkers, geologists, archaeologists, historians and naturalists, and has been designated an Area of Outstanding Natural Beauty.

The centre of Lydham is grouped round the crossroads of the A489 and the Shrewsbury–Bishop's Castle Road (A488), with a war memorial and a church set above the road level. Behind the church there is the mound of a medieval motte and bailey castle and a mill.

The church is a 13th century building in origin – it was substantially restored in 1885, but has some interesting features. The Oakeley family are recorded as Lords of the Manor from at least the 15th century until 1897 when the estate was acquired by the Sykes family, who still own Lydham Manor and much of the land in the parish.

Lydham has no shop, school or pub and depends on Bishop's Castle, two miles to the south for most amenities, including doctors' surgeries, chemist and post office. There are two large houses: Lydham Manor (the main house was pulled down in 1968 when the stable-block was converted as a dwelling) and Roveries Hall (built 1810). The rest of the village consists of farms and smallholdings, old cottages, some council housing and some new houses, mostly bungalows.

Most families have gardens and grow fruit and vegetables. The old tradition of whinberry (bilberry) picking on the hills nearby is still kept up. Many local children still play at the Newton as their parents and grandparents did, learning to swim in the river West Onny. As they get older, however, transport is a problem, particularly in the evenings – they are dependent on lifts from parents or friends to enable them to go to clubs, sports or any form of entertainment, in Bishop's Castle or further afield. Nowadays many people have to work outside the area, although the majority are still occupied in farming or forestry.

Parts of the parish, particularly the Roveries, are wooded and fine

106

individual trees have been noted (see Andrew Morton: *The Trees of Shropshire* 1986). The Lydham Manor Oak (over 12 metres in girth) is mentioned as the county's largest recorded oak and possibly the second largest in the whole country.

Lyneal & Colemere 🌿

Colemere is a very old village, and 5 picturesque thatched black and white cottages, restored and updated inside, are highly prized by their owners. A group of 7 cottages built in 1953 for farm workers are not now fully utilised, as few workers are now employed on farms.

The village is very quiet, but the Colemere Country Park around the mere is popular at holiday times, when families and nature lovers come to visit the mere and surrounding woodland to enjoy the wild life. Members of the Colemere Sailing Club and fishermen also enjoy the mere.

Beyond the wood runs the Shropshire Union Canal, formerly the major means of transport. The horse drawn barges carried lime and coal which unloaded at the old kilns, still to be seen in Yell Wood. They also took the farm cheeses to the market in Ellesmere.

The present church was built in 1869 when Colemere and Lyneal were part of the Bridgewater estate. The stone came from Cefn-Mawr – cefn sandstone, carried by horse and cart to Trefor and then by barge to Lyneal wharf and taken across the marshy land on a specially built road, to the site of the former church. Lyneal-cum-Colemere church unites the two villages, a beautiful avenue of lime and horse chestnut trees leads from the church to Lyneal.

Lyneal is one of the oldest villages in Shropshire. The earliest recorded name, Lunyal, may refer to crescent shaped fields in the area at that time. In the 19th century Earl Brownlow owned 1620 of the 1900 acres which made up the village.

The village school was originally held in an upper room at The Firs, approached by an outside staircase. This room is now the Methodist chapel. The present school was built in 1880 and now is in imminent danger of closure as the roll is down to 22 children.

Lyneal has two recently restored black and white cottages. Some of the farms have changed from dairying to arable in the last ten years. Lyneal Wood now produces potatoes to be used for crisps. Silage making has replaced haymaking on larger farms. Mechanisation in sugar beet has made the greatest difference in farm work.

Maesbrook 🌾

This is border country where the land was trampled alternately by English and Welsh feet. There has always been a strong Welsh influence in Maesbrook. The most obvious expression of this today is in the Welsh place names and names of farms e.g. Dyffryd, Pentra Perfa, Gwerny Crai etc.

The village has always been divided into two distinct parts. The upper part is not surprisingly the driest area, and has always had the higher population. The lower end of Maesbrook can be an extremely watery place, as reflected in the house names of The Moat and The Ark. The official routes of the water are the rivers Vyrnwy and Morda, which is fine when they are confined within their banks. For many years attempts have been made to control flooding. A system of argaes (earth banks) was devised to help contain the water. These it is thought were improved by Thomas Telford when he was County Surveyor. However several times a year lower Maesbrook is cut off by an impressive flow of water which deposits debris along the hedges as evidence of its passing.

Despite its nuisance value, the water has also been a means of livelihood. The fertile flood plain has supported agriculture and the river Morda itself two mills. Pentreheylin Mill was where farmers took their corn to be ground. Higher up the Morda was a papermill. It is believed that local people saved their hedge-clippings and rags to take there. Both mills are now private houses.

Religion has always formed a large part of the life of the village. For many years people travelled to the parish church at Kinnerley. However discontent with the traditional forms of worship led to the opening of two chapels in 1844. The Methodist chapel is still in operation, with the Sunday school being held in the original school room. The Baptist chapel went into decline and has recently been demolished. The village acquired its own church, St John the Baptist, in 1878.

In some ways there is continuity of tradition in Maesbrook. Many families have lived here for generations. Most livelihoods are based on the land as they always have been. At the same time there has been change. The closure of the village shop and post office came as a shock to all. It was sorely missed, being a centre of village life.

Maesbury 🐚

The village of Maesbury lies 4 miles south of Oswestry. A large part of the village is low-lying ground and because of this, the far end of the village is called Maesbury Marsh. Through this area runs the Shropshire Union Canal, which in the old days served a coal-wharf, a bone works which made glue, a grain store and flour mill. In those days the canal was busy and the beautiful barges were looked after by families who became well known to the local people and much admired for their pride in their boats.

Most men were employed at the flour mill on the edge of the village, or worked on farms in the district. The mill was one of the first firms to use steam lorries, which delivered flour and animal feeds to shops in the neighbouring counties and was the first to use a bulk lorry, which was well known on the route to and from the Liverpool Docks.

There is a church and there used to be two chapels which were supported well, especially for occasions like Anniversary and Harvest Festival, which was always followed by a sit-down Harvest Supper. Entertainment was often in the form of a Social Evening, which included fancy-dress, dancing, games and local acting – and the sight of two young lads dancing together in their heavy boots was something to remember!

At the far end of the village is St Winifred's Well – a local place of interest, where sick pilgrims went for a cure.

At one time there were two shops and several pubs, but only one shop and two pubs have survived. There were originally two schools, one Church and one Chapel, and great rivalry existed between them. The pupils from Chapel were called the 'Marshybikes' and the Church children were the 'Chainybikes', the names derived from the location of the schools. The Church school was called the Chain School as it was adjacent to Chain Lane, which had a toll house. The Chapel School was situated in the Marsh. In 1923 a new County School was built which replaced the other two.

Mainstone 🐚

Hidden within the remote and beautiful hills of south Shropshire, on the ancient rampart of Offa's Dyke, Mainstone remains essentially a close knit farming community.

The church of St John the Baptist, the Church on the Dyke, is well worthy of attention. The Victorian restoration of 1887 thankfully preserved its best features including a magnificent Elizabethan oak roof structure and its history has been traced back almost 400 years.

The inhabitants of Mainstone work hard and enjoy their leisure hours together, obviously bonded by a shared love for the surrounding hills and beautifully wooded landscape that dwarfs the few cottages and scattered farms. Their sense of history is equally strong, the huge boulder in the church weighing 230lb, a constant reminder of its long, firm roots. The village derives its name from the Welsh Maen meaning stone. A legend tells of the building of the church, originally intended for a spot closer to the village. Every night the stone, reputedly a relic of the Ice Age, mysteriously moved to its present site nearer the Dyke and eventually the villagers resigned themselves to building it there. The ground on which the church now stands was given by King Charles II for kindness shown to him by the people of Mainstone during one of his escapades.

Marton 🐾

Marton, in the parish of Chirbury, is situated 16 miles south west of Shrewsbury and 7 miles from Welshpool on the Welsh border. It has a population of about 300.

Farming is the chief occupation, but there are also two builders and a carpenter in business in the village, and at one time there was also a blacksmith. Most of the young people travel to employment in Shrewsbury or elsewhere.

The houses of Marton are of different periods, some modern and others very old. There are black and white half timbered houses, some of these dating back to 1634. St Mark's church, which is built of stone, was erected in 1855.

The Church school was built in 1864 and was closed by Shropshire County Council in 1948. In protest at its closure, a rebel school was run by parents for three years, salary paid to the teacher being £3 per week. The school was re-opened in 1951, and was again closed in 1984 due to falling numbers of pupils. Marton children are now taken to Chirbury Primary School. The school premises have since been sold.

In 1890 the village post office was opened. Before this the village had only a letter box. For the past 150 years the village shop has been run by the same family.

Marton Pool

Marton has two public houses, the Sun Inn, in the centre of the village, where many years ago minor court cases were held, and the picturesque Lowerfield Brook or Marton Pool Hotel, which has a thatched roof and where they once brewed their own beer.

Perhaps the most outstanding feature of Marton is the Mere, known locally as Marton Pool, which used to cover 30 acres, but now covers considerably less since drainage. About fifty years ago a Roman boat was found in mud around the pool. This boat is now in a Shrewsbury museum. It is from the Latin word Mereton meaning lake or pool, that Marton derived its name.

Overlooking the village is Marton Hill, where a small cottage known as Bray's Tenement was the birthplace of Dr Thomas Bray (1656–1730) English clergyman and philanthropist.

Meole Brace 🌿

This once idyllic hamlet has become suburbanised, but the atmosphere and community spirit of a village remain.

The old part under the shadow of the church still has great charm, in particular Church Row. The Manor, Meole Hall, has never been listed among the stately homes of Shropshire. The grounds contain the site of the castle burnt down in 1669, erected by the De Braceys, Lords of the Manor in the 12th century. From them comes the name Brace. Meole is hill, mill or sandy bank.

From the bend in Vicarage Road, passing School House garden with its gnarled walnut, where owls nest, one used to be able to see the cemetery and distant spires of Shrewsbury. That view was dramatically removed in 1933 when the by-pass sliced its way through the heart of the village, demolishing a favourite pub, The Red Lion, and one of the earliest cast iron bridges in the country, designed by Telford as part of his London-Holyhead Road. Modern estates now crowd in on the old heart of Meole.

Mary Webb, the Shropshire novelist, lived locally. She was married in the village church and is buried in the cemetery, beneath a simple white cross.

Middleton 🌿

The parish boundary of Middleton encloses a cross-section sweeping from the upland common with its prehistoric stone circle to the fertile valley in which a new tied cottage has recently been built next door to the site of a medieval moated farmstead.

The origin of Mitchell's Fold, a Bronze Age stone circle, is found in one of Shropshire's favourite folk tales – the story of the Witch and the Fairy Cow. This tells how the villagers suffered so greatly in a period of drought and famine that the fairies took pity on them and gave them a magic cow. This would give them milk as long as they obeyed the rules:

'It shall not fail if but one pail
Each wife shall daily draw.'

All went well until the local witch took a mischievious hand. She milked the poor creature into a sieve which, of course, never became full. This so enraged the good fairy folk that the witch rapidly came to an untimely end, imprisoned in the stones of the Fold.

Tiny Middleton, with only a dozen houses, widely scattered, is unusual in having two Halls, the seats of the two former lords of the township, as its official designation used to be. That this is an ancient division is shown by the 1086 Domesday survey.

Disruptions all along the Welsh border in the 12th century made farming a hazardous occupation. In Middleton, Medgley's Moat is a good example of the fortified holdings which were built along the Severn valley.

On Middleton Hill, where the Victorian tithe map shows 'the Warren', the delicate Mediterranean rabbits originally introduced to England by the Normans were helped to survive the rigours of the Shropshire uplands by a series of artificial burrows, now described as pillow mounds.

The most important recent development of the village was in Victorian times, with the building of a church, vicarage and school, plus adjoining schoolhouse, to cater for the needs of the rapidly increasing number of workers in the local mineral mines.

Since the closure of the mineral mines, depopulation has caused the sale of the vicarage and school buildings as private houses. Services at the church now only occur on a rota basis, as the parish shares a vicar with neighbouring churches.

Minsterley ✎

The name Minsterley is derived from the name Menistrelie and means either the minister or the chapel in the forest clearing.

After the Norman conquest, a manor house was built and the village sprang up around that. Until 1920, the parish was owned by the Marquis of Bath and his predecessors, but then was sold and the manorial rights elapsed.

Agriculture was always the main source of employment, although around the late 1800s to early 1900s, mining provided a small amount of work. Present day employment in the village comes from a variety of sources, the largest being Express Dairies Ltd.

Up until the middle of the 19th century, the village was self-sufficient. Nowadays the village has only one general store, a post office, newsagents, a fancy goods stores and a pottery. People tend to use the major shopping facilities in Shrewsbury, a market town 9 miles away.

Religion played an important part in people's social lives throughout the century and Minsterley still boasts 3 well-attended churches today. The Holy Trinity Church was actually completed in 1689.

The Crown and Sceptre pub is of particular interest. It is a beautiful black and white building, built in 1240 as a private home, becoming a pub in 1840. The Bridge Hotel used to be called the Miners' Arms and the Bath Arms, formerly The Angel, had its name changed in honour of the Marquis of Bath, hence the coat of arms currently hanging over its threshold.

The annual Minsterley Eisteddfod, a very popular event drawing people from a large area, is held in the parish hall and has been since it was re-started in 1963. Another big date on the calender is Minsterley Show.

The population in Minsterley has trebled since the beginning of the century and is still growing as new houses are being built.

Monkhopton 🎵

Monkhopton parish consists of three small communities, these being Monkhopton, Weston and Great Oxenbold. The present inhabitants are mainly connected with agriculture, it being purely an agricultural area.

The church of St Peter's is situated just off the main road in Monkhopton. It is a small red stone Norman building dating from the 12th century. Opposite the church is Monkhopton House, a large red bricked building with half of it dating from the 17th century, when it was built for the third son of the then Earl of Wenlock, who was a monk, hence the name Monk in front of Hopton.

Monkhopton had a small village school from 1849 until its closure in 1983. It is now a private house. There was a public house at one time, but this was closed down about 100 years ago due to being over patronized by the Irishmen who were building what is now the main road. The hostelry was called the Wenlock Arms and although it is now a farm-house the coat of arms can still be seen above the front door.

Up until the Second World War Weston consisted of just two farms with one double cottage and a turnpike. The turnpike or tollhouse means that this was once a rather important highway. Then during the war four agricultural dwellings were built, and later Weston had the addition of two bungalows and a private house.

To the south west of Weston is Great Oxenbold, once a small

114

monastery connected to Wenlock Abbey. The present building is only part of what was once a much larger construction. The Great Hall and Chapel are now a farmhouse, the village has long gone, but there is one new bungalow. Most of the woodland has been felled and the last deer disappeared about 25 years ago. The great fish ponds no longer exist.

Montford Bridge & Montford 🐟

The traveller on the A5 trunk road west of Shrewsbury will hardly fail to notice the village of Montford Bridge, for it is here that the road crosses the bridge over the river Severn, the river which virtually divides Shropshire into two halves.

Montford Bridge and Montford (a hamlet about a mile south west of Montford Bridge) formerly formed part of the Powis estate. When it is considered that Powis Castle is some 20 miles away, one can visualise how large many of the old estates were in days gone by.

St Chad's church, serving both villages, is perched on a prominence at Montford, and can be seen for miles around. It is built of local sandstone with a square tower. In the churchyard are two family vaults of Charles Darwin's family, although he himself was buried in Westminster Abbey. Montford and the adjoining village of Shrawardine, share a vicar, who lives in a modern house adjoining the church, the original rectory now serving as a high-class restaurant. A mile long bridleway connects the two churches, and many riders and ramblers enjoy this area which abounds in wildlife.

The children no longer have their own village school, but attend Grafton and Baschurch. Until a new village hall was built in the 1950s, village activities used to take place in a small room in the yard of the Wingfield Arms public house.

Proposals are in hand to by-pass the village by the early 1990s in order to ease the holiday traffic problem to and from North Wales. This will no doubt be of great advantage to many residents.

More 🐟

Few strangers find the village of More unless relatives are buried there or they are searching for fossils!

The present day village surrounds the 13th century church, which is on a circular raised site with huge stones in the walling that suggest pre-Christian consecrated ground. The site of a wooden castle can be seen as a raised area in a field named Moatlands, with a line of mounds for houses of the original village.

There are about 42 habitations in the 3,500 acres comprising the parish of More. Living here are the families of smallholders, farmers, workers on farms, in forestry, local food processing, agricultural trades, the cattle market, market gardens, Bishop's Castle's shops, and retired folk.

Linley Hall is an 18th century Palladian house, designed 1742 by architect Henry Joynes of London. One needs to look carefully from each point of the compass, to realise this is not a simple foursquare house; each face is unique, and stands very little altered outwardly since 1760.

Morville ☙

Morville nestles under Aston Hill between Much Wenlock and Bridgnorth on a site continuously occupied since Saxon times. The Norman church replaced a Saxon building mentioned in the Domesday Book. Two women and five horses were killed by lightning as they left the consecration ceremony in 1118.

Standing close by, Morville Hall, a National Trust property, is closely associated with the church, being built in 1546 on the site of and using stones from Morville Priory which had become derelict during the Reformation. Built as a traditional Elizabethan house it was extensively altered in the 1750s to its present Georgian style. In 1961, the South Pavilion, formerly stables was converted into a Pack Holiday House and many Brownies, mainly from inner city areas, stay there each summer.

Morville still retains two ancient monuments. The whipping post, standing on the junction of the Shrewsbury and Craven Arms roads, was regularly used according to parish records. The Pound, recently rebuilt, stands in the corner of the Acton Arms car park. Filled with soil many years ago it supports the small bus shelter, built to commemorate the Coronation in 1953.

Facing the church, across the meadow, stands the Acton Arms public house, built originally as the Abbot's lodgings for the Priory, and reputedly haunted by Richard Marshall, 28th Abbot of Shrewsbury who once lived there.

The Acton family, a very important Catholic family from Acton Burnell, were first recorded in Morville when Edward Acton MP for

116

Shropshire built a house at Aldenham in 1383. The beautiful wrought-iron gates at the main entrance, came from the Great Exhibition at Crystal Palace in 1851. Legend says that the replica of an armoured leg, dripping blood, above the gates, belonged to an early Acton who cut off his own leg, then threw it across the stream to claim ownership of the land on which it fell.

The school, an important focus for any village, has remained open and progressive despite much reduced numbers.

Munslow & Aston Munslow 🖎

Both Munslow and Aston Munslow are connected with the Baldwin family, who once lived at Aston Hall and have a commemorative plaque in Munslow church.

In Aston Munslow, places of note are the White House which dates back to 1400 and is now a rural museum, and the Swan Inn, a lovely old building where Dick Turpin is supposed to have stayed. In the village there are still traces of an arbour drive, up which deer, caught in the Long Forest, were driven centuries ago. Agriculture is still the main source of employment in the area. Sometime in the latter half of the last century, the first Hereford bull to be exported from England to South America was sold by Mr Richard Shirley of Baucott Farm.

In Munslow village, St Michael's church dates back to 1115. It is recorded that from 1776 to 1965 the living was in the same family, the Powells, who succeeded each other in direct line. A Powell relative who served in the Navy brought back a stone from the Great Wall of China in the last century – it was set in a wooden holder and used as a doorstop for the south door.

The only non conformist place of worship still open in the area is the Methodist chapel at Aston Munslow built in 1862.

The local hostelry, The Crown Inn, is of great historic interest having once been a Hundred House.

Muxton 🖎

The settlement of Muxton between Lilleshall and Donnington, grew up around the dwelling of the swineherd to the Manor of Lilleshall. The name comes from Mocs (pigs) and tun (house).

When the mines and quarries were being worked in Lilleshall, a canal spur linked them to the Marquis of Stafford's canal which ran between Pave Lane and Donnington Wood. The Lilleshall spur was 70 feet lower than the main canal so barges were taken up a tunnel to where two shafts had been dug beside the upper canal down to the roof of the passage; loads were transferred between levels in box-like containers.

In 1790 the tunnel was abandoned and a small inclined plane was built and used for almost a hundred years to transport coal and limestone by boat to the Lodge Furnaces. These huge furnaces produced the finest pig iron ever made, they closed in 1888 and only the remains of the foundations are to be seen now on The Common at Donnington.

At Muxtonbridge a beam engine pumped water from the mines into the canal, the ruins can still be seen in the woods.

Around 1888 the spiritual needs of the growing workforce were catered for by the provision of several corrugated tin Mission Churches. St John's church in Muxton Lane is still in use today but St Chad's Mission Church which served the miners of Granville Colliery has been removed from Lodge Bank and reconstructed at Blists Hill Museum in Telford.

With the coming of steam powered engines the railways superseded the canals and a mineral line linked Granville Colliery to Donnington Station. The new pedestrian subway with its 'Halley's Comet' tiled mural has been built at the old coal wharf.

The nearby brick chapel is now an orthodox church used by the Serbian community which became established here during the Second World War. Next door is a house with the unusual name of 'Treasure Trove Villa', so called because a hoard of Roman coins was discovered during excavations for the foundations of the house.

Mytton

Mytton, a small community of some 24 dwellings, is divided between the parishes of Fitz and Montford. It is bounded by the river Severn and divided by the river Perry. Both rivers have in the past been important as the means of transporting iron ore, which was mined in an area known as Bromley's Forge. A small wharf was built just off the Severn where barges could be loaded and taken to Ironbridge.

Mytton Hall stands on the site of an earlier farmhouse dating from the 18th century and some parts still remain. A previous owner began a small school around 1880 in a building close to the river Perry. The building still exists though now extended as a private house.

Mytton Mill is situated between Fitz village and Forton Heath beside the river Perry. The business was founded in 1897 by William Wall Timmins and was used commercially to grind barley using water power.

The Mill operated throughout the Second World War. Afterwards, it was taken over by Allied Bakeries who ran it down and it finally closed in 1966. The premises were then sold to Onions and Rowley builders, who now have their Head Office there. Due to their enthusiasm for the preservation of old buildings and machines, the Mill has been adapted to give new life and purpose to the area. Today, Mytton Mill is a centre for several light industries, including glass decoration and woodturning.

Nantmawr ✧

The village of Nantmawr lies not far from the Welsh border a few miles south of Oswestry. There is a lovely view of the Welsh hills as one descends the two hills leading to the village. The name Nantmawr means 'nant' brook and 'mawr' big. A small brook, hardly a big one, meanders through the meadows surrounding the village.

At one time Nantmawr was a thriving community surrounded by quarries and there was even a brickworks. Now the post office, the shop, the United Reformed Church with school have all gone.

There used to be an inn in the village called The Carvers Arms. A wood carver owned it and there is still a carved cupboard door in one of the rooms.

The first quarry here was started by a Mr Savin from Trefonen. The coal was taken by horse and cart down Coal Lane to fire the lime kilns below Nantmawr. A conveyor belt was used to take the stone from above the village to the kilns. There were six kilns 30 feet high. Stone was loaded into trucks as much as a man could handle, for which he was paid 8½d a ton. It was then broken up again by the men working the kilns and they were paid 6d a ton. The worst job of all was taking out the lime from the bottom of the kiln and wheeling it along an 11 inch plank. They were paid 3½d a ton for this. As they sweated the lime burnt into their feet, backs and arms until they were agonisingly red-raw. At times, such was the demand from farmers for lime, the quarry worked day and night with the trucks queueing up to take it away. The quarry had various owners until, with the advent of the new fertilizers, demand for lime dropped and the quarry at Nantmawr closed. There are still two large quarries below Nantmawr, one for concrete making and one for road filling.

Nantmawr is now a quiet, friendly, residential community with a mixture of young families and retired people.

Nash

In the Domesday Book Nash was known as Esses, which means 'At the Ash Tree'.

Also mentioned in Domesday is Hulla known now as 'Court of Hill', Nash. In 1683 most of the present house was built by Andrew Hill incoporating an earlier 13th century house. The Hills and their descendants lived at this house until 1927.

The chapel, or church as it is now, is of the Decorated period although rather plain. The windows are said to be original, most of them now are of stained glass including a good example of modern work. There are no very old monuments or gravestones in the churchyard due to the fact that before 1884 all burials took place at the mother church in Burford.

Next to the church is the large brick house called Nash Court which was built in 1760 by the Arbuthnot family and is now a school for boys.

On the other side of the church, in the field once known as Bell Court, was built Nash School in 1846. It was enlarged but in August 1958 closed due to difficulties in obtaining a running water supply and the decline in the number of children attending.

About ½ mile to the east by the roadside stands The Great Oak of Nash. It is over 450 years old.

The post office was closed in 1979 and the red telephone box was removed at the same time. There is still a collection box and daily deliveries of milk and newspapers and the Mobile Shop calls twice a week except when Nash is snowbound.

The majority of traffic down the lanes these days is tractors, bailers and combine harvesters. Farming, mainly milk and cereals, is the main source of income. Some people travel to local towns for work and quite a number of inhabitants are retired folk.

Alas there is no longer a cricket team but activities like churchyard mowing and fund raising events are well supported by all.

Neenton 🐟

Neenton, originally called Newentone in Domesday times is situated on the river Rea.

Many little water mills were situated on the Rea and Clee Brook, the most noteworthy being Charlecote just two fields into Aston Botterell parish. There was an iron smelting forge, the ironstone being brought from Bouldon by pack animals. The pig iron was extracted and sent on to the Round Thorn, by the old road through Neenton and Bridgnorth and on to the river Severn.

In the 19th century, the Lyster family owned over 900 acres and by this time the village was 1,132 acres. They were patrons of the church and in 1871 a new church was built on the site of the old one. The estate was sold in 1913, the nephew keeping the patronage. In 1986 this was passed to the University of Cambridge.

The Harley family lived at Brook Cottage for 100 years, they were coopers and made barrels for the homebrewed ale at the New Inn (renamed the Pheasant in this decade)

Hall Farm was cruck built about 1400. Major Smallman, a local Civil War hero was born and bred at Hall Farm. As a Cavalier pursued by Roundheads he rode straight over Wenlock Edge. He was caught by the trees but his horse fell to its death. This place is now known as Smallman's Leap.

Neen Savage 🐟

Neen Savage is a small parish lying in the south east corner of Shropshire very near to the border with Worcestershire. The river Rea runs north to south through the parish. The name Savage is said to have come from Adam de Sauvage, a friend of Ralph de Mortimer who was granted lands in this area by William the Conqueror.

This area has always been predominantly agricultural, though in years past there were a number of industrial workings, probably the oldest being the brick kilns at Overwood. The corn mill at Detton, the paper mill at Paper Mill and a Lyd Mill which is believed to have stood just above Titford Bridge, all flourished in the 18th and 19th centuries. Blacksmith's forges could be found along the river; within living memory there was a blacksmith at Bell Vue and also an aerial ropeway bringing

Dhu stone from the Magpie Quarry on Titterstone to Detton Ford station.

After the Second World War the need for the mills and other industries gradually ceased and the parish became totally agricultural. The Cleobury Mortimer-Ditton Priors Railway used to run alongside the river Rea through the parish but this closed in 1965 and the land has been returned to the various farms.

With no pub or shop, the focal point is the church. Situated opposite the vicarage, now privately owned, the church of St Mary dates back to the 12th century. A tower at the west end was topped with a wooden spire which was burnt down after being struck by lightning in 1825.

Just over 100 houses scattered over 4,400 acres make up the parish; some new, some restored and some converted. There are 8 Paper Mill Cottages and in 1948 10 Council houses were built at Barbrook. One of the oldest unaltered houses (still no water or sanitation) must be Cherry Orchard, a half timbered building with no foundations, said to be of the 11th century.

Since the closing of the school in 1964, and partly because of the amalgamation of so many farms which has resulted in the selling off of the farmhouses to commuters, who follow diverse occupations outside the parish, the community spirit has not been as evident as it was once. However, in an effort to remedy this, after many money raising events organised in the parish, the new Parish Hall has been built on glebe land, next to the church, which was purchased from the Diocese of Hereford in 1984.

Nesscliffe 🎋

The name Nesscliffe comes from the Saxon word Ness meaning a promontory.

Nesscliffe and nearby Hopton Hills have been quarried for many centuries to provide building stone for homes, farms and castles both locally and elsewhere. The quarry faces that survive are a vivid reminder of those times and bear the carved initials of some of the workmen. Set into one of those faces is Kynaston's Cave, a dwelling hewn out of the rock. It has two rooms and is reached by a worn flight of stone steps cut out of the solid rock. The infamous Humphrey Kynaston is believed to have sheltered there and was notorious for his many exploits including murder and robbery. He died in 1534; the date 1564 inscribed on the cave is believed to have been added later. An old seat carved into the stone beside the fireplace in the Old Three Pigeons Inn is reputed to have been used by Kynaston and an account of his misdeeds hangs nearby.

Around that same time history records that the chapel situated at the foot of the hill had fallen into disuse. Attached to that church was a hospital or almshouse. On the foundations of those buildings there was erected in 1754 a Charity School. This was rebuilt in 1870 and survived until 1969 when it was replaced by the present school.

The railway was last operated by the War Department from 1941 to 1960. The army still has a large training area on the edge of the village and the noise of gun and mortar fire is often heard. Their helicopters too are a frequent sight and sound.

But probably the greatest influence on Nesscliffe today is the London to Holyhead road which still cuts through the village with its incessant traffic. At peak holiday times crossing the road is very difficult and dangerous but one farmer still manages to drive his dairy herd to and from their pastures without mishap. The traffic on the road helps to provide business for the service station, the hotel and the village shop. It also brings custom to the cottage garden nursery and homes providing overnight accommodation.

Newton

Newton is a hamlet in Stokesay parish nestling on the banks of the river Onny.

Some of the houses are half timbered, with decorative chimney pots of local stone. Others are built of a warm golden coloured stone quarried locally.

It was a self-contained community at the turn of the century, most people being self-employed, and thus all facilities for everyday living were available. There was a blacksmith's shop, a cooper, an undertaker, a coalman, a stonemason, a milkman, a butcher, a carpenter, a grocer, a post office and even a resident policeman. The Red Lion Inn of the same familiar stone with a thatched roof was demolished in the 1920s.

A Baptist chapel was built in Newton about 1872 through the influence of the Lord of the Manor, John Darby Allcroft. In the early 1900s the chapel became a social meeting centre, and eventually the headquarters of the local branch of the British Legion Club. It has now been converted into a private dwelling.

123

This quiet backwater of Newton has remained largely unchanged over many years, maintaining its own identity in spite of the fact that it now adjoins the much larger settlement of Craven Arms which grew out of a railway junction.

Nobold 🌿

Nobold is a small, chiefly farming, area in the parish of Meole Brace. Nobold, formerly called Newbold, is a derivation of the words New Buildings, and at one time had a considerably larger population than it has now.

Nobold's history dates back to Roman times. A Roman road can be traced through Meole Brace, along Mousecroft Lane and finally along a footpath in the direction of Hanwood from whence it went to the Roman camp at Caer Flos. There were two toll houses, both in Longden Road.

The only transport for the residents of Nobold prior to the end of the First World War was a carrier's cart. The first bus, in the early 1920s, was a small brown affair known as 'Bogey-Jones'. There were steps up to the door at the back and passengers sat on a continuous seat around the bus with market baskets being stacked in the middle.

The industry of Nobold included clay and gravel pits, a brickyard and kiln, and a blacksmith. Mr Atherton owned coal-pits in a field opposite Sweet Lake Cottages – a row of 8 cottages on Longden Road, built at the turn of the century. Two deep shafts were sunk sometime prior to the First World War. These were brick lined and underground was a narrow road with rails thereon for the tubs. The sides of the tunnel were supported by pit-props and the pit-head equipment included an engine shed and lifting gear. The men, who were poorly paid by piece-rates, worked only by the light of tallow candles and at times it was very dangerous. The yard coal was hauled up and stacked at the side of the road.

One site in Nobold Lane of particular interest is Conduit Head. This was a spring source called Broadwell which, it is recorded, supplied water to Shrewsbury from 1556. The value of the Conduit Head to the local heritage of Shrewsbury has long been recognised, and in 1987 a project to create a combined visitor centre and historic site was opened.

Norton in Hales

Sixty years ago the village boasted three public houses, one butcher's shop, a general stores, a clogger, a laundry and one old lady who used to put comfrey dressings on cuts and bruises. Today there is only one pub and a general stores/post office.

All this is in great contrast to the time of the Domesday Book, in which the village is named as Nortune, meaning 'north farm in the meadows'. The present church, St Chad's, was built in the Norman period by Herbert fitz Helgot.

A glacial boulder, known locally as The Bradling Stone, stands in the middle of the village green. One legend suggests that this marked the boundary of the parish and, on the occasion of Beating the Bounds, the younger members would be bumped on the stone so that they would remember the parish boundary. Another version suggests that anyone found working on Shrove Tuesday afternoon or other holy days was bumped on the stone as a punishment. A use for the stone was found earlier this century when itinerant teams of farm labourers (after taking refreshment in the local inn, then known as The Griffin Arms, now The Hind's Head) would challenge each other to fights, the stakes being placed on the Bradling Stone.

In a field at Norton Farm stand two strange stones, one perpendicular with a hole in the middle and one upright, called the Devil's Ring and Finger; legend has it that infants were passed through the ring in order to cure illnesses.

Until Dr Beeching's axe fell, there was a single-track railway line, which was opened in 1860 and linked Market Drayton with Stoke on Trent. The station and station-master's house are now private dwellings but evidence of the railway can still be seen from the bridge. Special trains used to be run from Stoke bringing large crowds to Norton in Hales for the annual harvest home festivals; following an afternoon church service, a meal was provided under canvas in the grounds of the rectory and the Market Drayton Town Band played.

The village has a thriving Jubilee Hall and a sports field with facilities for cricket, bowls and tennis. As the farms gradually employ fewer people, the majority of the residents commute to the towns to work, so diminishing rural life, but the community spirit is still strong.

Onibury 🌿

On the A49 from Shrewsbury to Hereford lies the village of Onibury, nestling in an emerald setting of meadows and woods in spring, and gold in the autumn.

The flaw in this jewel is that it is cut in two by the road, railway, river Onny and bridge. The larger part contains the church, school, post office and stores, nursing home, village hall and Onibury farm. Thatched cottages enhance the village, built of local stone with delightful gardens.

The church is old, having a list of incumbents since 1066 and Norman architecture prevails.

Onibury has changed considerably over the years. The coming of the railway brought new residents and new jobs. The station has now gone, electricity has replaced the old paraffin lamps and tallow candles. Tapped water has been a godsend, villagers no longer do their washing in the stream – this has been piped underground. Agriculture no longer finds work for the labourers and their cottages have been replaced by council houses in the towns where the workers go to factories. There are no large families now and the population has diminished.

Oreton 🌿

Aerial pictures of Oreton show a pattern of smallholding-sized properties bordering the common land. Agriculture in Oreton is carried out on a smaller scale than in the neighbouring villages, often supplementing some other source of income. Oreton was, for a long time, part of Stottesdon parish, but it was transferred in 1877 to Farlow, and there are now many links between the two villages, including a shared village hall. An ancient Bronze Age settlement at Lower House is nominally in Oreton, but is separated from most of the village by one of the area's notorious 'banks'.

Oreton is, and always has been, less dependent on agriculture than its immediate neighbours. Since Roman times there have been limeworks in Oreton, and quarrying too. Oreton Marble was used in the building of the Catholic church in Ludlow. Neither the quarry nor the limeworks is active today, though there are still folk around who remember fetching 'a pennyworth of lime' to whitewash the house, and there are houses named The Limes, The Claypits, and Limeworks Cottage.

Many houses in the village lie, not on the public roads, but down some very rough private lanes. Even the public roads are not wide, which may explain the popularity of one of the present day industries; car body repairs! This lies down Factory Lane. One researcher has found evidence that the 'factory' which gave this lane its name was in fact a cotton mill. Cotton was brought in by mule from Prescott. The site by the Rea Brook would certainly have provided enough water.

While there was plenty of local work, the retail trade was well supported too. Local residents recall Mrs Keys from the butchers at the top of Oreton Bank, and some with longer memories recollect her mother there too. There was a bakers at Summerfield. Both these businesses have gone now, and the shops are private houses. The village shop/post office is also a bakery, and for those that cannot get to the shop, they run a mobile grocery van, which can be relied upon even in the worst of weather. With a petrol station next to the shop, most essentials can be obtained in the village.

Pant 🖉

Pant, (said to mean 'the hollow under the hill') lies in the borderland between Oswestry and Welshpool on the busy Manchester to Swansea trunk road.

In 1841 it was recorded that the township of Crickheath contained the hamlet of Pant, a mountainous area with limestone quarries. The hamlet consisted of 8 or 9 stone cottages, a Congregational chapel and the tavern; other cottages were scattered around the hillside. Local families owned and worked some of the quarries, the stone being used for roadmaking or burnt in the kilns to make lime for the land. These kilns can still be seen by the canal side. Trucks loaded with stone came down tramways which crossed the road in two places and continued down to the canal. One of the gin wheels which controlled the trucks can be seen by the Clifton Cafe. This has recently been restored to almost its original state.

The Montgomery canal came through Pant and was used to transport lime, coal, stone, grain and other goods. One horse towing a boat could pull a load of about 20 tons.

A breach higher up the canal occurred in 1936, this was never repaired so the canal fell into disuse and was officially closed in 1944. While water remained in it the scene along the towpath was full of interest, wild flowers lining the banks, water fowl and swans nesting, dragonflies in abundance. This once beautiful area is now a jungle of briars. Plans are being considered to open up the canal as a tourist attraction.

Changes have come in the last 40 years. Many of the original stone cottages have been altered or demolished, the policeman with his bike has been replaced with patrol cars, roads are improved, footpaths laid, a main water supply came from Sweeney Mountain Reservoir, electricity arrived enabling the Parish Council to provide footway lighting.

The village has a bus service, three general stores with a post office and cafe. The area is a paradise for naturalists, birdwatchers, walkers, climbers and archaeologists. With a population of over 1100 Pant is no longer a hamlet!

Picklescott 🌿

The village which can also be spelled 'Picklescote', is situated in a hollow, 4 miles from Church Stretton on the lower slopes of the Long Mynd at its northern end. It is easy to see how it developed on this crossroad with a stream running through it. Picklescott is on a direct easy route over the northern slopes of the Mynd. Many a weary traveller must have welcomed its hospitality before tackling the Long Mynd. So the village grew and changed over many hundreds of years.

In those days Picklescott boasted a blacksmith, with the smithy making its own horseshoes, a grocer's shop, a toll house, a carpenter's shop, which was also a wheelwrights and an undertakers. There was a public house at the Gate House, The Gate Hangs Well. At one time there was also a beerhouse at Top House Farm. Picklescott even had its own school at the Vandals, but with the building of Smethcote School in 1864, the old school became a farm. The field opposite is still called the schoolyard.

Picklescott was a village of farms with 7 farms within its boundaries. Until the outbreak of the Second World War almost all the villagers worked on the land or in trades essential to the farming community. Life was hard, working hours were long.

The water supply from Adam's Well can no longer be used for drinking or cleaning dairy equipment. The reservoir at Adam's Well was built by Mr Walker of Batchcote Hall. He donated this to the village and had the supply piped to a conduit in the centre of the village. Before this, a few farms had their own donkey-tail pumps over wells outside the back door. Others used brook water for household chores but drinking water was carried from the Port well outside the village. Many a lazy boy, sent with his wooden yoke and buckets to fetch fresh drinking water, would stop to play and dip his buckets in the brook and go home innocently with his freshly drawn load no-one any the wiser, not a trick to be tried today!

Electricity came to Picklescott in 1936. The power supply was taken from Buildwas power station over the hill above Picklescott to service the barytes mines at Cothercott and Huglith. These mines provided work for some of the village menfolk who were no longer needed on the farms once mechanisation was introduced.

Pontesbury 🐝

Early maps show the name as Pantsbury or Pansbury, which roughly interpreted from Welsh means 'settlement in a valley'. The valley is provided by the oddly shaped Pontesford Hill, whose elephant-like form can be seen for miles around. There is evidence of two castles in Pontesbury but the settlement grew as a mining community, being conveniently situated between Shrewsbury and the iron mines of the Bishop's Castle area.

St George's Church, Pontesbury

129

St George's parish church, an impressive building set in the village centre was originally built in the 12th century and rebuilding was done in 1825.

Pontesbury Church of England School was built close to the church in 1760, a huge stone building which served the community until 1961. The site in the centre of the main one-way street now houses a nest of small County Council dwellings for older residents together with accommodation for their warden. Many of these residents spent their early days in the school!

The Comprehensive School was named after one of Pontesbury's most famous inhabitants – Mary Webb. Author of several novels, Mary Webb lived at Roseville, Hinton Lane, Pontesbury. Whilst residing there she wrote *The Golden Arrow* using a local legend as her theme.

Of more recent years Pontesbury people are proud to have shared the village with Miss Lily F. Chitty, a most remarkable lady who died in 1979. She was awarded the OBE and Honourary MA as an acknowledgement for her services to archaeology. Her family leased an area close to Pontesford Hill which was developed as Shropshire's first Nature Reserve. Now called Earlshill Nature Reserve it attracts many visitors. The main feature of the reserve is an old barn which has been restored and fitted out as a visitor and study centre.

Present-day Pontesbury is a dormitory village with little local employment. The village has developed in recent years from a small rural settlement employed in agriculture, quarrying and mining. Over the last 30 years housing estates have developed and inhabitants now come from various parts of the country, many retired people choosing the peaceful convenient Shropshire village to settle in.

Porthywaen 🌿

Porthywaen, the name means 'gateway to the common land', is situated about 4 miles from Oswestry on the Oswestry to Llangynog main road.

The area is rich in minerals, lime and granite still being quarried. On the nearby hill there are caves once mined by the Romans for copper, zinc and lead. Years ago several small lime kilns were privately owned.

The limestone was burnt in the kilns and then loaded onto small rail trucks which were drawn by horses and taken to the nearby wharf to be unloaded. Farmers from near and far would then collect the lime, now in powder, which was spread on the fields and gardens as a dressing.

Housewives also used the lime to whitewash their homes, both inside and outside the houses. The workers in the lime were nick-named 'Lime Dusters'.

About 1920 a businessman bought all the kilns from the owners and now only one large lime quarry remains, owned by the Steetley Lime Co. which provides much of the local employment. On the Steetley land, near to the quarry, there was a coal wharf and a blacksmith's shop.

In the early part of this century there were three public houses, a flourishing grocery shop including a corn merchants, in Porthywaen, selling home baked bread, home cured ham and bacon, farm butter, eggs, many items of clothing and footwear, and a chemist department, and two butchers shops.

In the early 1930s, the Porthywaen Silver Band was formed. It has been very successful, winning many prizes in competitions. The Bandsmen and their friends built the Band Hall.

Porthywaen railway station was closed years ago, but part of the railway line is still used for wagons going to collect the granite from the nearby Llandu Quarry. The Primary School built in 1839, on land given by the Earl of Powis, was closed in 1985. The pupils now attend the newly built 'Bryn Offa' School in Pant.

Prees 🌿

Prees is considered one of the finest examples of a Saxon hill village, one of only two identified hill villages in Shropshire.

Its name predates the Norman Conquest and has been defined as being the derivative of the old British word Pryswyd, interpreted by the Saxons as brushwood. The heaths skirting the village today exemplify this and the name Prees Wood survives on the perimeter of the village.

Documented evidence, although scant, has a Collegiate Foundation of Monks at Prees in Saxon times and St Chad's the parish church would seem to stand as a monument to this first foundation.

Manor Cottages, once a single yeoman dwelling of cruck construction based on a mid 15th century open hall is known to have been the home of the Steward of the Manor, witnessed at least one Court Leet, been a farmhouse and housed the head gardener of Prees Hall. Legend has it that a 30 foot well to be found in the garden is linked to St Chad's by underground tunnel.

The 'Lock Up' still stands at the rear of the Constable's House. Built in the 18th century of sandstone ashlar with heavy cornice and slab stone roof with ball terminal at the centre, it is one of only five such structures known to be in existence in England today.

Prees retains a garage but gone is Grindley's Motor Cycle Depot although the 'Grindley Special', designed and built by the then owner, is remembered for its entries in the Manx T.T. Races.

In 1829 the principal trade was malting, not surprising with ten outlets for alcoholic beverage at that time. By 1841 a variety of occupations are identified and apart from the predominance of farming, shoemaking and brickmaking rated high followed by tailoring and estate related work. Industry remained scattered until the advent of the Salopian Cattle Bowl Co. some 50 years ago and from this beginning developed the industrial estate of today.

Deemed a Conservation Area, with a by-pass imminent, Prees should be assured its village status for future generations.

Preston upon the Weald Moors ⚜

The parish and small rural village (formerly 'on the Wild Moors') is located 3 miles north east of Wellington, just outside the Telford New Town boundary.

The village was mentioned in the Domesday book as Presture or Priest's Tun. The latter name suggests that the village may have been under ecclesiastical ownership before the Norman Conquest.

In 1336 the independent church of Preston was established. Little is known of the old church. The present church is dedicated to St Lawrence, and was built in 1739–42.

Preston Hospital, now known as Preston Trust Homes, was founded in 1716 by Lady Catherine Herbert, daughter of the first Earl of Bradford. She left £6,000 in her will to build and endow almshouses in Shropshire, in thanksgiving for her rescue by one of the famous St Bernard dogs, when lost in the Alps. Built in 1725 to house 12 widows and 12 girls, it was extended and improved at later dates.

The oldest house is Hoo Hall, called Howghe Hall in 1612. This black and white timbered house was probably moated in the Middle Ages.

The Shrewsbury canal and the Birmingham and Liverpool Junction canal – Newport branch, both passed through the parish. The canal keeper's cottage, next to the school, is near the site of the canal bridge. This was destroyed in August 1985 as part of engineering research,

132

prompted by national concern about the effects of the increasing weight of traffic on old arch bridges. Residents fought to save the bridge, but to no avail. The winding pool, near the bridge, can still be seen, although the canal was last used in the 1940s, and was partly filled in by 1970.

Industries in the area included salt works, sand extraction and a brickworks. A windmill was noted, ½ mile west of the village, in 1676. Although one or two alesellers were licensed in Preston in the late 18th century, no later premises are known, and the village is still 'dry'. However the Queens Head at nearby Horton is within walking distance.

Farming is still an important part of village life, but hardly any farm workers live here. Most residents work outside the village, so that Preston has become a commuter village, with the church and school trying to hold the threads of the village community together.

Pulverbatch

Pulverbatch stands 9 miles south of Shrewsbury 600 feet above sea level, rising to 1300 feet on Cothercott. The village is spread in pockets among the hills with a population of about 400.

A ditty written by a local in about 1770 shows that Pulverbatch village has always been divided into very definite areas.

> Cothercott upon the hill
> Wilderley down in the dale
> Churton for pretty girls
> and Pulverbatch for good ale.

Cothercott is the area that rises high overlooking the Stiperstones range. It is wild in winter but with wonderful views over the countryside. The area supports hill farming. It lies quiet now with only old mine shafts and spoil heaps to give evidence of the copper and barytes mines worked here in the past. The barytes ore was processed at the foot of Cothercott hill, a narrow gauge rail track was constructed to the brook so the ore could be easily washed. The mine across the valley at Huglith hill used an aerial ropeway to carry the ore across to Malehurst for processing.

Wilderley has the remains of an old motte and bailey castle, but not such a fine example as the one across the valley at Castle Pulverbatch, known locally as the Knapp. Its outlines are clear to see and a climb to the top of the mound shows what a good defensive site this was. This castle was still occupied in 1205 and the village was an important stop

133

Pulverbatch Village

for the drovers walking the Long Mynd. It is in Castle Pulverbatch that you will find the village post office and the two public houses, The White Horse and The Woodcock.

Church Pulverbatch is the correct name for the whole parish and also refers to the part of the village where the church stands. It has been known locally as Churton since the 13th century. One of Churton's pretty girls was a lady who lived to the grand age of 101 years. She was Mrs Mary Ward who kept up the tradition of giving away Soul Cakes on All Souls Day. She was a member of the Jaundrell family, a family responsible for the building of some fine large buildings in Churton. Another of the Jaundrells still appears in the form of a ghost frequenting the Beech Bank between Churton and the Wilderley road.

The farms today are family businesses which on the whole do not employ outside labour. Many of today's inhabitants are retired, the others commute to work outside the village. The local children travel by bus to schools at Longden and Pontesbury, Churton's school being closed some time ago.

The village comes to life at the pubs, the village hall functions, and in the shop and church. Elsewhere life is quiet, take a stroll along the lanes and footpaths and you are in unspoilt rural Shropshire.

Quatford 🦡

Situated on the A442, 2½ miles south of Bridgnorth on a bend of the river Severn, there are a few houses on the main road but the nucleus of the village is set on either side of steeply winding Chapel Lane which continues through lovely chestnut woods to meet up with the Stourbridge Road.

Overlooking the village at the top of 33 steps is 900 year old St Mary Magdalene church. Near the church is an ancient oak tree, identified on the Ordnance map as belonging to the pre-Conquest period and a relic of the original Morfe Forest.

The Village Hall is built of brick and is approximately 150 years old and during this time has served as a chapel, stabling and a home for displaced persons.

Very little new building has been done in Quatford, which really remains much the same as it has been for years, but cottages have been reconditioned and renovated. In 1960 when the A442 road was widened the vicarage, schoolhouse and three cottages were demolished.

Until 1940 there was a ferry at Quatford. The parish of Eardington on the opposite side of the river was joined with Quatford and they used to ferry the parishioners over for church services. This has now ceased as the boundaries have been altered.

The waters of the river Severn are rented to the Birmingham Angling Association. During the fishing season many of their members are to be found lining the river banks at weekends. They seem to find much pleasure enjoying their pastime in the peace of the lovely countryside.

Ratlinghope 🦡

Ratlinghope is a village with a low density population, lying under the eastern slope of the Long Mynd. Its name means 'valley of the children of Rotel'.

Ratlinghope became a Priory of Augustine Canons in the 12th century and was a cell of Wigmore Abbey. The present church has two main claims to fame. The first is that up to a few years ago it was heated by apparatus, surmounted by a Crown, once used in Windsor Castle. The second is that it was the indirect cause of the Rev Donald Carr, in 1865, being lost in the snow on the Long Mynd for 22 hours as set out in the little book entitled *Night in the Snow*.

Many years ago there was a small brick works in Ratlinghope and several properties in the area were built with these local bricks, unfortunately not of a very high quality. There has also been a Corn Mill. The Mill Cottage is still standing today.

Ratlinghope has its own geological rock system known as 'Ratlinghope conglomerate' comprising 'quartz pebbles set in more or less compact red sandy matrix'. It is a popular area for geologists and field study students. Over the years a number of ancient tools have been found together with some Roman coins. There is evidence of tumuli and a British camp.

Ratlinghope is a hilly area only suitable for grazing sheep and a few cows and for many years its inhabitants have earned their living from farming. In common with many country villages, the land will not support so many people and jobs other than farming are continually being sought in nearby towns and cities. There is still no mains water or drainage in Ratlinghope and apart from a recently organised mini-bus service once a week to Church Stretton, there is no public transport.

It is designated as an area of outstanding natural beauty.

Richards Castle 🐚

Richards Castle is an unusual village with a castle, two churches and two parish councils – because the Shropshire/Herefordshire boundary runs through the parish!

It was Richard fitz Scrob who gave his name to the village. He built his castle here in 1065 on a good defensive site facing the Welsh border. Walk up the steep hill to this castle and you will discover St Bartholomew's church to the east of the castle bailey with its detached bell tower overlooking the land below. Inside you will find a church barely touched by the 19th century, let alone the 20th century, with box pews, a musicians' gallery and the hatchments of the Salwey family who, to this day, are the resident Lords of the Manor of Richards Castle.

There are many interesting and attractive buildings in the village, some timber framed, others built of locally quarried stone, but pride of place must go to the beautifully restored medieval stone dovecote. Once the home of 600 pairs of doves, it now serves as a maternity unit during the lambing season.

The 4,871 acres of Richards Castle parish extend from the steep, wooded hills on its western boundary to the water meadows along the river Teme in the east. The topography has dictated the economy of the village over the centuries with the emphasis on forestry and stock-rearing.

In 1873 Moor Park, one of the two great houses in the village, was sold to Major Johnston J. Foster from Yorkshire. He died in 1888 and All Saints Church, the 'new church', was built in his memory by his widow. The architect was the famous Sir Richard Norman Shaw.

In recent years Richards Castle has lost many amenities: the railway, part of the bus service, the post office, the village shop and finally, three years ago, the village school. Nevertheless, the village is a thriving community of 640 people with many activities, most of which are centred on the well cared for village hall.

Rodington ✤

A village between Wellington and Shrewsbury, deriving its name from the river Roden.

The church (now St George's) was mentioned in the Domesday Book, but it was rebuilt in the 18th century and again in the 19th century, so that the beauty of the smaller church has been lost.

At Rodington the Shropshire Union Canal was carried over the Roden in a triple semi-circular arched brick aqueduct. This, as well as several picturesque draw bridges have since been demolished. The main wharf for loading and unloading was opposite the entrance to Rodington House.

The Bull's Head is reputedly the second oldest licensed house in the county. Adjacent to it was the Bull Ring, where bull-baiting and also cock-fighting took place before 1840.

There are still several farms but many local trades are now extinct and most people commute to jobs outside the village.

Rowton (nr Cardeston) ✤

Rowton, an enclave between the parishes of Cardeston, Alberbury and Wattlesborough, was originally the estate belonging to Rowton Castle and as such more or less self sufficient. It consists of a cluster of farms, houses, a pub and a castle.

The castle dates back to Roman times. In 1482 it was razed to the ground by Llewellyn and rebuilt through the ages, the present building being early 19th century rebuilt by the Lyster family, who owned the estate for several generations. In the 1940s the estate was sold. The castle became a blind school and eventually the Royal Normal College for the Blind, until 1978 when the college moved to Hereford.

The bulk of the agricultural part of the estate was sold to Mr Silcock whose family had made their fortune through animal food manufacture and his descendants still own it. Various small properties have been sold off over the years. The cottage where the rabbit catcher lived for instance, and others where estate workers were housed are now private houses, although there are still some estate houses retained on the now reduced Rowton estate.

An old windmill survives without its top from which the nearby Windmill Inn probably takes its name. This house proudly stands on the brow of the hill at the highest point of Rowton, still carrying on its trade through surrounding changes. The castle premises have altered greatly. The students' accommodation buildings are now luxury flats and the assembly hall and swimming pool is now a sports club complex, while the castle itself is emerging as a hotel.

Rowton (nr High Ercall) 🌿

It is on record that, in 1086, Routone had a priest. The present sandstone church of All Hallows was built in 1835, and is a perpetual curacy, now in the care of Rev David Rogers of High Ercall.

The granite obelisk, standing on a grassy triangle in the centre of the village, is visited by people from as far away as the USA. It commemorates Richard Baxter, 'author and eminent citizen of the 17th century'. Richard declined the Bishopric of Hereford and, after the Act of Uniformity, threw in his lot with the nonconformists, and was cruelly treated by the notorious Judge Jeffreys.

His monument is overlooked by a beautifully restored timber framed Elizabethan cottage. Of the other 20 or so homes in Rowton only three appear to have been built this century. Sometime ago the buildings of the wheelwright and the blacksmith's shops were incorporated into a small cottage, making a commodious house.

Rowton used to boast a Halt on the GWR line, but Dr Beeching's axe put paid to that in 1963 and the lines were removed in 1967. The bridges built to carry roads both under and over the lines are, after 120 years, in wonderful condition. A real credit to their builders. The skip owners are now very busy filling in the cuttings with rubbish, and when it is consolidated and covered with topsoil, the land should revert to the farming land from which the line was carved by the navvies, with their shovels and barrows all those years ago.

Rushbury 🐝

Rushbury village nestles under the Wenlock Edge, in the picturesque south Shropshire valley of Apedale, appropriately named 'The Valley of the Bees', because of all the bee-keeping done in the area by the monks of Wenlock Abbey in the 13th century. Rushbury is unique, in so far as it is the only village bearing that name in the country. The name means 'The Rushy Forte' and this suggests that it was a fortified place during pre-Norman times. From the entry in the Domesday Book it appears that Rushbury (under Riseberie) was a fairly prosperous settlement.

St Peter's church, an early Norman church with Anglo-Saxon herring-bone masonry by the north doorway, stands at the highest point of the ridge of the land in the village. On Shrove Tuesday children of the village school do 'Clipping the Church', by linking hands to encircle the church with their backs to the building, and then walking sideways around it. Evening celebrations take place in the village hall at Wall-under-Heywood, where pancake races and competitions are enjoyed by old and young alike. In October, the community decorates the church to celebrate Harvest Festival with a service and harvest supper.

The school is the centre of activity in the village. It was built and endowed by Benjamin Wainwright in 1821, together with two alms-houses and a schoolmaster's house, which are now incorporated into the school.

'Wall Wake' is celebrated in July on St Margaret's Day – 'The Eve, the Day and the Morrow', when activities include a barbecue, a sponsored walk and a party for all the children in the village hall.

At the edge of the village, there is a brook and a medieval Pack Horse Bridge which carries the footpath up the steep bank to Wenlock Edge. It is possible now to drive up Roman Bank to gain superb views of the village or study the varied wildlife in the area.

Rushbury itself may be quite a small village, but the parish, where farming is the main occupation, covers over 5000 acres, and extends some 5 miles along Apedale, and although scattered has a great community spirit.

Ruyton of the XI Towns 🐝

Ruyton of the XI Towns, which lies midway between Shrewsbury and Oswestry, was once a borough town and is mentioned in the Domesday Book. It gets its name from the 11 townships which are:- Ruyton, Coton, Shotatton, Shelvock, Eardiston, Wykey, West Felton, Haughton, Rednal, Sutton and Tedsmore. A plaque showing these townships is fixed to The Cross, a stone monument erected on the site of the old Lock-up.

The village is in the parish of the church of St John the Baptist. The church was built by the Normans circa 1120. The remains which can be seen in the churchyard are of a castle, built in 1155 and demolished by the Welsh in 1403.

The war memorial is unusual in that it is a cave hewn out of the red sandstone rock. On the rear wall, a cross has been carved and on the side is a tablet bearing the names of the men of the village who fell in the two World Wars.

The river Perry runs through the village and it was across this that Platt Bridge was built in 1701. It was built by a local builder whose designs were seen and passed by Thomas Telford. It is said that the head carved on the side of the bridge is that of Telford himself. On the other side of the river is a toll house and it cost 1 penny to cross the bridge.

Ruyton used to be self-supporting with its own local craftsmen. The farms supplied the milk and butter. The villagers used to work on the farms or at the brickyard situated at Olden Lane and owned by Mr Brown of Ruyton Hall.

During the First World War, a group of farmers led by Mr W. H. Gittins of Hall Farm formed a Farmers Co-Operative Dairy to produce Cheshire Cheese. In 1915 they moved to the present premises in School Road. In 1936 it was taken over by Krafts and in 1954 by Express Creameries, the present day owners. Today this is the major employer for the area.

St George's

St George's was formerly called Pains Lane. It is now within the eastern boundary of Telford, but retains its village atmosphere.

The first Pains Lane church was a wooden structure which was burnt down, and replaced by a brick chuch in 1805. The present stone-built church was erected in memory of George Granville, 2nd Duke of Sutherland and consecrated by Bishop Lonsdale on 10th October 1862. An oak tree was planted surrounded by iron railings to mark the spot of the old church. At a public meeting at the George Hotel, it was unanimously agreed to change the name of the village. This was when St George's was born.

The Lilleshall Company brought industries into the district. In 1861 they brought their engineering works to Gower Street under the name New Yard Engineering Works.

In the 1800s there was a racecourse at the southern end of Pains Lane. This comprised of School Street, Goulbourne Road, and London Road. The grounds of the Grove were used as a paddock and the grandstand was on high ground in School Street.

Terrace houses at St George's

141

The Recreation Ground was granted to the village by the Lilleshall Company at a cost of £500. Money was raised by public efforts. It had a quarter mile cinder track for cycling and foot racing and was the finest track in the Midlands, having Olympic Trials held there.

The Lilleshall Company played a big part in the public life of the village. They built houses and allowed a Church of England School (now closed), the Village Institute and St George's Youth Club to be built on their land at nominal rents.

St Giles with Sutton 🐚

Sutton is situated just 2 miles from Shrewsbury. Sudtone, as it was in Domesday Book, lay close to Rea Brook, which provided water for its mill.

In 1848 it was said that Sutton had changed little in 600 years. It still had a small church, a mill and 5 farms, with about 700 acres owned by 'Baron Berwick'.

Downstream of the mill, Sutton also had its own spa, the care of which was entrusted to the occupier of a cottage on the spot. It was said of the water that a 'tumbler glassful operates as a brisk aperient'.

Sadly, very little of the old village remains. Though Spa Cottage still exists, the mill has gone and its only remnant is to be found elsewhere in the parish.

As for the little Norman church, its bell last rang at the end of the Crimean War and its remaining wall forms part of a farm's barn concealed behind modern bungalows at the southern end of Sutton Farm Estate.

The Severn Valley branch of the old Great Western Railway was built over Rea Brook and Mill Race and across the open land separating Sutton and St Giles. Now its tracks are removed the western side has been made into a good footpath, whilst the Council have planted the eastern stretch with wild flowers. Much of that open land is now built upon and as Springfield Estate has taken on the name of the large house that previously stood there.

At the other end of the parish, a 17th century milestone marks the entrance from Shrewsbury to the village that grew up around the red sandstone church of St Giles, which stands today in a peaceful church-yard with almshouses under its wing.

The formation of Shrewsbury and Atcham Borough Council in the 1970s brought the two villages into the same council area. Modern developments have merged their boundaries and since the 1980s, the two parishes have been combined. The new name sounds right for a parish that still retains village features and an identity quite separate from that of Shrewsbury Town.

St Martin's 🌿

For over 50 years St Martin's was a mining village. It is situated between Oswestry and Ellesmere, and 3 miles from the Welsh border. The colliery closed in 1968, and there is now a small industrial estate at the old Second World War prisoner of war camp.

The village has two schools, Ifton Heath Primary School, and Rhyn Park Comprehensive. There was St Martin's Church of England School, but this closed in 1953. The building is now used partly as a church hall and the doctor's surgery.

The Miners Welfare Institute was built in the 1930s and was maintained by weekly payments from the miners' pay packets. It is now the village hall, and is used by all the village organisations. The old colliery mounts have been developed as recreational sites with an old coal truck as a memorial.

The Shropshire Union Canal runs through the outskirts of the village, and carries a great number of holiday boats to Llangollen from the Midlands. Years ago miners and farmworkers would spend summer evenings on the canal wharf playing marbles, quoits, and meggy. Meggy was a piece of wood sharpened at both ends hit into the air by another stick, and teams took part in the game.

The oldest building in the village is the parish church dated in the 1150s. The tall box pews, and three tier pulpit were removed in 1980, but the pulpit and one pew are being restored at the back of the church. By the church gate are the old almshouses, now modernised only on the inside, and now owned by the council. They were originally built as a school for 12 poor female children in 1810 by the Viscountess Dungannon. There is also a Pinfold where stray animals were kept until claimed on payment of a small fine.

Sambrook 🌿

In the Domesday Book Sembra was the name given to what is now known as Sambrook. Sambrook is situated ½ mile from the A41 and has

143

always been agricultural but has changed its character greatly with the passage of time. There is now one dairy farm and a stud farm in the centre of the village and a kennels breeding gun dogs.

Within living memory the village was self sufficient with a blacksmith, wheelwright, tailor, shoemaker, post office and shop and even a slaughterhouse to its name. Earlier there are records of a mason and a baker in the village which also had its own brick kiln. There was a forge on the pool at Sambrook with two water wheels which worked the bellows and hammer. It is said that these could be heard for several miles.

The present mill was built in 1853 and was run for many years by Miss Nock who lived in the sandstone house opposite the mill. Miss Nock undertook the running of the mill upon the death of her father when she was 20 years of age. The mill supplied many local farmers and families with flour and grain, the grinding wheels being driven by a water wheel powered by the water from the pool. This mill was in use until the death of Miss Nock in 1975 at the age of 79. The mill has now been converted into a quite unique home with the water wheel having been completely restored.

In 1838 a small chapel was built by subscription but was never consecrated. However, baptisms took place there and the little iron font now stands in the churchyard. This chapel could not be used for marriages or burials and in 1856 the present church, vicarage, school and schoolhouse was built at a cost of £3,724 using local stone and craftsmen. The school, which took 70 children, was later moved to what is now Sambrook House. The former building was bought by the villagers, after a great deal of fund raising, and converted for use as a village hall.

The old shops and businesses in the village are now all private houses. A small number of new houses have been built and old barns converted into homes. The public house continues to thrive. With the creation of Telford New Town and the building of the motorway network, Sambrook is now populated largely by business people who have chosen to live in the peace and tranquillity of this interesting village.

Selattyn, Pantglas & Hengoed 🐚

The land between Wat's Dyke and Offa's Dyke holds 3 villages – Selattyn, Pantglas and Hengoed.

Above Selattyn rise the Selattyn hills, reputed to have sheltered that mystical man of myth and legend Owain Glyndwr, the wily adversary of

Church of St Mary The Virgin, Selattyn

Henry IV and Henry V. These hills surround the area on one side, and the massive Bronze Age earthworks bordering Hengoed stretch along the other.

The 3 small villages share several things in common, the principal one being the church of St Mary the Virgin, Selattyn, parts of which date back to the 13th century.

Many things here testify that it is border country, the area knew constant skirmishing and fighting in centuries past and soldiers' graves can be found at the side of the Dyke marked by stones. The penalties for being found on the 'wrong' side of Offa's Dyke were high for English or Welsh, but there is evidence to suggest that here between the two dykes was some 'common ground' where trading could take place. Many roads and lanes cross through Selattyn and undoubtedly people met and went about freely in this area between any pitched battles. Also there are several little lanes and paved trackways – hidden unless looked for, suggesting they were put down for the use of mounted men travelling to and from a large fortification, now long gone. One theory is that the Romans used these trackways, but mystery shrouds their origins.

Pantglas originally housed the estate workers for Brogyntyn Hall, Lord Harlech's country house. The Harlech family built and funded the school here, but this has now been converted into private dwellings, as has the estate laundry building.

On the edge of Pantglas there is a marshy wood where alders grow. Nearly every year this would be visited by a clogger who made piles of clog soles from the alder wood.

Hengoed's little church of St Barnabas built by the Reverend Albany R. Lloyd in 1850 was (controversially) demolished in 1985.All that now remains is the burial ground with a commemorative plaque mounted on the original font standing in the quiet grassy clearing where the church once stood.

Hengoed is not so much a village as a community. There are no village name plates on the approach roads to Hengoed, which mystifies strangers. Locals know it is divided into Lower Hengoed, where the churchyard is and where a water mill used to be at Park Mill farm; Middle Hengoed, where there is a lane rejoicing in the name of City Lane, and all the houses have 'tree' names; and Top Hengoed which has the pub, The Last (meaning a cobbler's last), the post office and shop.

Shawbury 🐝

The village of Shawbury has occupied its present position on the North Shropshire Plain since Saxon times. The name of Shawbury means 'the fort in the trees' and in those early days a moat surrounded a fort. It stands on the river Roden which supplied the moat and supported a mill and several forges in the vicinity of Shawbury. Sadly nothing remains of these nowadays.

This fort, surrounded by the moat, would have been a wooden structure occupied by the Lord of the Manor. Only the site remains now to remind us of former days. This site is now preserved, the moat being considered the finest in Shropshire.

The church too had Saxon beginnings when it too would have been of a wooden construction. The present stone building is of Norman origin, added to and rebuilt many times in its long 900 year history.

Agriculture has been the mainstay of life over the ages with a strong rural community remaining to this day. Although, at one time, the majority of Shawbury villagers would have been involved in agriculture, today sees many and varied occupations among the inhabitants.

William Hazeldine the famous ironfounder was brought up in the district. It was in his iron foundry in Shrewsbury that the links and chains for the Menai suspension bridge were tested.

The RAF station was established in 1916 when the Royal Flying Corps built an airfield on the edge of the village. Since then it has blossomed and grown and is now a major helicopter training station. The RAF personnel live in and around Shawbury adding to the character of the village.

The houses are a mixture of old and new, the old part of the village remaining round the church and on the main road. Several large houses are known to have been pulled down to make way for modern dwellings and now several modern housing estates stand where big houses once graced the landscape. Today Shawbury is a thriving community with several shops, post office, bank and public library. The parish hall is in constant use for many public and private functions.

Sheriffhales

Sheriffhales is a small village situated halfway between Newport and Shifnal on the B4379. Approached from Newport the traveller is afforded the only birdseye view of the village from Hilton Bank. Going down into the village one passes the only remaining blacksmith's workshop. Mr Eardley is a farrier as well as a general blacksmith, serving local farmers as well as shoeing the horses in the vicinity.

The present centre of the village may be considered to be around the village shop and post office. In the last 50 years this area has been developed to provide housing for families and elderly people. As public transport has declined, the importance of the village shop has grown.

The more ancient part of the village surrounds the church. Facing it is a lovely timbered Tudor cottage, still owned by a village family. On the opposite side of the road, on a small hill, is the church of St Mary's, which in summer can be glimpsed through the beech trees. In the autumn they provide a spectacular colour display. In 1981 the Duke of Kent planted a copper beech here to commemorate the Queen Mother's 80th birthday. The church building dates from the 13th century, with later additions.

Past the church two small lodge cottages stand at the entrance to what was at one time claimed to be the longest lime avenue in the country. The Manor House has a history dating back to the 16th century. At some time it was the home of the sheriff of this village, which was then simply called Hales. In the years after the Reformation there was an academy here for those Catholics barred from attending university. The manor is now run by Slater Farms, which owns a large part of the land surrounding the village as well as farms elsewhere. The late Mr Slater built up an Ayrshire herd which now has a worldwide reputation.

Shipton 🌿

An impressive mansion is the focal point of Shipton. Shipton Hall is believed to have been built in 1587 although this replaced a much older black and white timbered house which had been destroyed by fire. It was said to have been given by the owner of the neighbouring manor house, Richard Lutwyche of Lutwyche Hall, as a dowry when his daughter, Elizabeth, married Thomas Mytton and remained in the family for the next 300 years.

In the grounds of the Hall is a 13th century dovecote which has been very carefully restored to its former glory. A dovecote could only be granted to Lords of the Manor by a Royal Charter. There is a cave-like tunnel which leads from Shipton Hall to Larden Hall, where it came up in front of the fireplace in the main hall. Larden Hall was sold in the 1960s and was shipped stone by stone to Disneyland, in the United States of America, but the tunnel still remains although only a few hundred yards are still passable. It was thought to have been used as a means of escape in troubled times to find sanctuary in the church of St James, which is found in the grounds of Shipton Hall. The church dates back to Norman times although the chancel was rebuilt by the son of the original builder of the hall.

The village of Shipton has moved from its original site, which was on the field now known as Bakewell Yard in front of the Hall. One of the original owners of the Hall did not like his view being spoilt by his servants' homes, so had these knocked down and replacement ones built a little further up the dale. One of the original buildings still stands. The Bulls Head was once a pub and butcher's shop and the hooks on the wall for hanging the meat on can still be seen.

The Hall has always played a major role in the lives of the people of

Shipton. During the Second World War, whist drives were held at the Hall to raise funds for the war effort and when the soldiers were de-mobbed £5 was given to every man returning to the area. The rest of the funds were put towards the cost of a village hall to be erected as a memorial to the fallen of the Second World War.

Shrawardine 🌿

Six miles west of Shrewsbury on the A5 trunk road is a turning to Shrawardine – Shra to rhyme with 'way', war to rhyme with 'war', dine to rhyme with 'mine'. However, the inhabitants have no problem – they settle for 'Shraden'.

The village is set upon a hill, overlooking the river Severn as it leaves Wales and meanders around Shropshire. Standing guard on the hill is the small sandstone church of St Mary which has a lovely view across the plain to the Breiddons. The remains of Shrawardine Castle are in a field opposite. Both the original church and castle were destroyed in 1645 during the Civil War. The church was rebuilt, but the castle is now just a small pile of stones, most of the remainder having been used to repair Shrewsbury Castle and the wall on Severnside.

Scattered over a wide area are some 40 homes, and in common with most villages these are occupied to a large extent by people who commute to work in Shrewsbury and elsewhere and retired people. In 1932 the Council purchased one large farm and this was divided into smallholdings, affording a living for some 9 families, and this arrangement exists today.

One cottage in the village known as Court House, had large cellars in which luckless offenders of the law were confined, and it is said that an underground passage from the cellars ran across to the castle. Subsequent to its being used as a prison, Court House was burned down but was afterwards rebuilt and still bears the name used in harsher times.

There is no public house, shop or school (the children being bussed to Grafton and Baschurch) but there is a tiny post office, dealing with pensions and postage stamps. The Shraden village 'hut' which had seen many happy social gatherings was sadly closed in the 1960s and part of the timber construction is now doing service as part of a cattle shed at Broomfield! For social occasions nowadays, Shraden shares a village hall with the village of Montford.

Smethcott 🌿

A quiet village that lies on the flanks of the Long Mynd, with glorious views over the Shropshire plain to the north, the Church Stretton hills to the east and the sunsets over the hills of Wales.

Smethcott was built around the church in medieval times. The main road, or track as it would have been, ran from the Long Mynd to Shrewsbury. The village today lies to the east of the church, and has altered little since the 18th century. Two farms remain today, in the centre of the village.

Mobility and changing economics have brought different inhabitants to the village. In the past, there was employment in the neighbourhood, a poultry farm, the school, the roads, the railway, the Creamery at Dorrington. Now it is only the farmers and their families who work in the village, commuters travel further often to Telford and Birmingham. In the last 15 years 3 houses have been built all connected with agriculture.

Smethcott has no village hall, public house or shop, these are in Picklescott a mile away. The school at Smethcott was used for fundraising efforts and had provided a focus in the community but it was closed in 1964.

The family run farms are mainly stock with some corn, and even with quotas, milk production is the main livelihood. This milk is taken daily to Minsterley Creamery by tanker, the last collection of churns for Dorrington Creamery being in the late 1960s. The cows are Friesian, producing beef calves using Hereford and Continental bulls. A Suffolk sheep flock is kept in the village, with progeny sold at breed sales. Flocks of breeding ewes are a common sight on the farms around the village.

Smethcott church, standing on a rise above the village, dates from the 12th century. It was rebuilt in 1849, with a fine hammer-beam ceiling, the work of William Hill, a woodcarver from Smethcott Common. The church is cared for by a voluntary group of parishioners.

Two pools provide an ideal habitat for plants, waterfowl, kingfishers and herons. Smethcott Pool, about an acre in size, is opposite Pool Farm. The smaller Ben's Pool, reputedly named after a local blacksmith, is near to Corner Cottage.

Sidbury 🌿

Sidbury is a tiny community, some 6½ miles from the town of Bridgnorth. Its present day population is only 40 adults and 21 children. There is no shop, post office, school or pub, and no public transport other than the school bus. In spite of the isolation, however, all houses have mains electricity and either private or mains water, and most have the telephone. There is a post box! The main employment is in agriculture, with 8 farms, devoted to the raising of cattle, sheep, corn and roots. The estate woodlands provide work in forestry and gamekeeping and there are also trout ponds.

Despite its small population, Sidbury is interesting because of its history. The church is of Saxon origin, 'modernised' in Norman times. It was partially burnt in 1911, and rebuilt. Although ancient, the church is still active, with prayers said in the church every day. The vicar of Sidbury is also vicar of four other parishes, but his home is the modern vicarage in Sidbury. There is a tapestry map illustrating Sidbury at present in the Victoria and Albert Museum. A photograph of this map can be seen in the church. The old vicarage, complete with glebe land, was sold by the church, and is now the one farm in Sidbury not owned by the Reed family. The only other house not now in their possession is the beautiful old manor house of Hawkswood.

Sidbury, or Sudbury, signifies the South Burgh or fortified enclosure of Saxon times. The original moated castle stood on the site of the present Hall Farm. It was destroyed by Cromwell in the Civil War, and later replaced by a house. This too was destroyed in its turn, with only the stable block surviving. It is said that it was burnt to the ground by a jealous wife.

Following the fire, the family chose not to rebuild, preferring to use the Dower House when visiting their Shropshire estate. The present Hall Farm was built in 1830. Sidbury Hall itself was built in 1904 as a shooting lodge, which was later enlarged when it became the family residence. Apart from the sale of a few farms, the estate has remained in the same family since 1469.

Snailbeach 🌿

The Stiperstones range of hills encompasses an area of outstanding natural beauty. Intersected with deep valleys, or dingles, the summit of the range is crowned with a series of outcropping rocks like some vast tiara. Lore and legend about here, such as tales of Wild Edric and his fairy wife Godda, whose wild phantom rides over the hill-tops supposedly presage war.

Of great geological interest, the area boasts a remarkable history of mining, particularly for lead and barytes. Apart from a few isolated farmsteads in the lower reaches most of the small hamlets, including Snailbeach, owe their origins to mining as do their attendant places of worship, public houses (some now private dwellings) and two schools (one now a Field Centre).

Snailbeach is perhaps the best known mining complex with its particularly rich veins of ore. Here, at one time, over 500 men were employed. Outstanding, upon the hillside is the Big Chimney, culmination of a bricked flue running from the distant smelthouse and designed to carry away toxic lead fumes. This is the second chimney on the same site, the first one blew down in a gale. A fascinating feature of the place was its railway system with little engines hauling trucks from the workings to the smelthouse and finally to the wharf at Pontesbury.

Following closure of the main mining in 1910 the Halvans Company took over, sorting and sifting through the immense spoil heaps. The white dumps, so much a feature of the scene, and often described as 'a lunar landscape' are composed of 'sludge' from the buddles or washing plant. Containing residues of toxic elements like lead, cadmium etc no vegetation has ever clothed them.

High above the old mine reservoir stands Lordshill Baptist Church, used as the film setting for much of Mary Webb's famous novel *Gone to Earth*.

Miners were great sports enthusiasts and, in former times, marbles contests were regularly held. The old Snailbeach White Stars footballers were noted for their robust play. The modern F.C. has featured prominently in junior leagues and still continues. Miners were also ever singers, 'Sing for lead, whistle for coal', being the slogan. Most local churches had their mixed choirs and the Choral Union and Snailbeach Male Voice Choir were each notable in their day, travelling far and wide to give entertainment as did the church choirs.

St Luke's church comes just within the boundary of Minsterley parish and is organised thereby. The Methodist Church is a remarkably fine edifice, stone-built and complete with inside wood panelling. Seats were specially designed to accommodate the top hats of earlier generations, with underseat fitments. Both the aforementioned churches have burial grounds.

152

At one time Snailbeach had three general stores and a post office. These no longer exist in that capacity, the nearest now being at Stiperstones.

Soudley & Heywood 🐌

One lady has vivid memories of winter in Soudley. When frosts were hard and deep, the ponds in the valley froze solid and proved a great attraction to local skaters and those from Church Stretton. What a thrill it was to be able to go to the normally unapproachable island. Fallen trees and jutting roots reached down into the depths beneath the ice. The crisp air rang with exciting shouts of enjoyment and shrieks of delight as skaters and pedestrians mingled in various activities to the sounds of a gramophone. As darkness fell they flocked to the bonfire on the island for baked potatoes. Alas, the pool has now been cleaned, the island bulldozed away and trees felled. The new pool never freezes as hard as in 1927!

Stanton Lacy 🐌

Stanton Lacy is now a very quiet village, although in the past it seems to have been a little more lively. Now there is a church, two large farms, two large houses and a huddle of cottages, against a delightful background of woodland and a patchwork of small fields with hedges. There is no pub or village shop, not even a lamp post.

St Peters church is on the left over the bridge. The old flood boards remain near to the churchyard wicket. Foundations of a first church date back to 680. The story goes that beautiful Pious Milburga, daughter of Penda, King of Mercia, was closely pursued by a Welsh Prince who was determined to carry her off. Having crossed the river Corve she prayed that the water might become an impassable torrent. Her prayer was answered and the pursuer baffled. In gratitude she founded a church on the spot of her deliverance.

Church Farm to the east is steeped with history and the farm buildings are listed. The approach is under the wooden archway of a loft with massive beams and a stable for 9 horses. At the rear of the house is a complete cider mill. The Old Vicarage, sold off by the Church Commissioners in 1968, is the only village house not owned by the Earl of Plymouth.

The school, founded in 1872 was closed in 1982, for too few local children. Now they go by bus to a larger primary school at Diddlebury. The old school is presently used as a workshop of restoration for interior design. Nearby the schoolhouse is empty. It has an interesting lead trough in the cellar, presumably used for salting pork.

For their social life the villagers travel up the hill to the village hall at Haytons Bent. In December a Christmas Show is produced, everyone has a chance to show off their talent. No one misses this excellent evening out. Another important event is the Midsummer Fun Day in the field behind the village hall. Children race and adults try their hand at various skills. There are plant and produce stalls, and delicious teas served in the hall. Occasionally there is a parish party with lots of fun and games – quizzes being the favourite – and a licensed bar! For the younger villagers there are discos, country dancing and barbecues. All these events are fund raising, mainly for the church and village hall.

Stanton Long 🌿

Stanton Long was originally a linear village on one of the principal routes across the Corve Dale but became somewhat isolated when part of the route was superseded by the Shipton/Morville turnpike road in the 19th century. It has a population of 120 and is primarily a farming community. Those not engaged on the land commute to nearby towns.

The church built in the 12th century was much restored by the Victorians but still retains its original door with its elaborate hinges and small closing ring. The passing of time has seen the loss of the Methodist chapel, post office and shop. There is no village school and children are taken to nearby Brockton.

Stapleton 🌿

The village takes its name from the great Steplewood of medieval times which covered the area from the church out to Moat Farm and over to the neighbouring parishes of Pulverbatch and Longden.

The church, dedicated to St John the Baptist, is believed to date back to the 13th century and is unique, in that it consists either of two buildings, one built on top of the other or of two storeys later made into one with the removal of the floor of the second storey. This is borne out by a remarkable feature of a piscina (a recess for washing Communion vessels) 11 feet in height in the sanctuary.

Richard Llewellyn Purcell Llewellyn was a generous benefactor in the village, as well as helping to provide the village hall he was responsible for the erection of the village Pump House in 1897. This was to commemorate the Diamond Jubilee of Queen Victoria, and supplied water to all the houses at that end of the village. Other houses had their own well until mains water was brought in. The Pump House was re-erected in 1977 to commemorate the Silver Jubilee of HM Queen Elizabeth II. Although the pump was no longer needed it provides an interesting focal point at the bottom of Pump Lane.

Until the outbreak of the Second World War most of the men were employed on the farms. Today the farms are family businesses run by father and son or sons. The four farms in the centre of the village were dairy and arable – today all the dairy herds have gone.

The village is without a shop or public house and the post office closed in 1958. The school was built in 1874 and that, too, closed in the early

The Pumphouse at Stapleton

155

1920s. The children now travel to Longden or Dorrington to attend school. The nearness of Stapleton to the A49 means it is ideal as a commuter village but despite this it has a very close-knit community.

Stoke-on-Tern 🐝

Stoke-on-Tern is a small hamlet situated midway between the villages of Hodnet and Wistanswick. It is flanked at one end by St Peter's church and at the other by Stoke primary school. There is neither a shop or public house, however there is a very good travelling shop owned by one of the local men, this calls twice a week and caters for almost every need.

Stoke-on-Tern is mainly an agricultural area which has survived two outbreaks of foot and mouth disease, one many years ago and one which many people remember just a few years ago.

On 23rd December 1853 Thomas Dutton was born in a cottage at Manor Gate Stoke-on-Tern and at the age of 9 the family moved to the old stone poorhouse at Stoke Heath. He became known as the Shropshire giant standing at 7'3" and weighing in at 23 stone, a man of extraordinary strength who became famous over most of Europe.

The church, which Tom Dutton helped to rebuild in the 1870s is on the site of the original church which has a line of rectors dating back to the 12th century. There is a group of Norman coffin lids on the grass by the tower.

The Reverend Rowland Corbet had the school built in 1870, and it was used as a place of worship during the rebuilding of the church. It has been greatly extended during recent years. It is very pleasant and modern, 'a hive of happy industry'.

Petsey Farm lies on the bank of the river Tern, a beautiful old black and white timber framed building. It had a very early Kempe window which has now sadly been removed.

Stokesay 🐝

Stokesay Castle, its Elizabethan gatehouse, the church and scattered cottages are in a valley, and nearby the river Onny rushes over a weir. An Iron Age camp on an adjacent hill is a reminder that this spot was favoured for habitation in distant times.

There is a hill on the opposite side of the valley and there is a legend which says that two giant brothers lived on the hills. Their money chest was kept under Stokesay Castle and they threw the key to each other across the valley. One day it fell into the pool beside the castle. A raven is said to guard the key and the chest but neither have ever been found.

The church is one of the few examples of church building in Puritan times. Two elegant canopied box pews occupy half the chancel. Here the Lord of the Manor could worship in seclusion. At the back of the church are some primitive pews with ledges in front – not for books but feet, as the floor was unpaved.

Concern for the villagers was shown by Roger Powell, who in 1616 bequeathed £10 for the poor and for the maintenance of a schoolmaster to teach the poor men's children. Subsequently a school was held in the church belfry – a dark and chilly place one imagines. The schoolmaster's desk remains and the money is still used by the school at Craven Arms.

Stottesdon & Chorley

Stottesdon is a rural village, small, but expanding. It has a mixture of housing, some modern, others, many of them farmhouses, much older, dating as far back as the 12th century. Council houses have been built since the 1940s and the latest are bungalows for senior citizens. The school was built in 1872 for 134 children. Today there are 32 pupils, but the building is larger! The school is used as a meeting place for village activities.

The church of St Mary is of Saxon foundation and has for its parish a very extensive district. It is a large church. The ancient font is one of the most elaborately decorated specimens of Norman art to be found any-where. Another notable feature is the Saxon tympanum over the old west door. Maintenance of a large church by a parish, which though large in area, is not so in population, always poses a problem. In 1987 the parishioners were working to raise £20,000 to repair the tower.

The village has a shop, by the Bull Ring and old blacksmith's shop. There are two public houses, a new doctors' surgery and a Methodist chapel. There is also a post office but, unusually, this is, and always has been, in a private house (not always the same one), so it is not easily found by strangers.

Chorley is by no means part of Stottesdon. It has its own post office, Baptist chapel and village hall. Until fairly recently there were also a butcher, a baker, a wheelwright and a blacksmith. The principal families

157

connected with Chorley were the Harriotts and the Crumps, and the latter family eventually came to own much of the village. They continued in Chorley for several hundred years, until the latter part of the 19th century. At this time much of the population of Chorley was involved in mining, and the remains of the colliery can be found in High Wood.

Tasley

Tasley has never had a shop, pub, or proper school. It does however have a lovely church which was rebuilt in 1841, after a fire, on the same site that has had a chuch since Domesday times. There is a Norman font, and, for many years, an ancient barrel organ was used to provide the music for the hymns. The parishioners must have got very tired of the music because it only played four tunes!

Tasley used to be a mainly rural community with 6 farms and cottages on the estate owned by the Acton family. Up until the Second World War there was an annual National Hunt race meeting, which is commemorated in Racecourse Farm and Racecourse Drive. Brickyard Cottages are built on the site of one of the village's unsuccessful attempts at industry. The brickworks didn't last long because the bricks were considered to be porous. However, the village hall, built in memory of Captain Acton who fell in the First World War, is built from them, and they haven't let in the wet yet!

After the Second World War attempts were made to mine coal, but this also proved unsuccessful. In 1945 the estate was broken up, which opened the doors to more housing development, and Tasley is now fighting hard to preserve its identity against the encroachment of Bridgnorth, the neighbouring market town.

Tibberton

The village, which was recorded as Tebriston in the Domesday Book of 1086, is bounded on one side by the river Meese, and on the other by the B5062 Newport to Shrewsbury road. Until 1912 Tibberton was part of the Duke of Sutherland estates and the tied cottages are a feature of the village although most are owner occupied now. There are some original black and white timber framed houses dating back to 1611 and all are in good order.

It is a rural village and farming in all its various aspects was once the main occupation, but many of the farms have ceased to be. Another source of employment at the beginning of this century was a paper mill on the bank of the river Meese but this ceased trading and in 1932 the last part of the mill, a large chimney, was demolished. This caused great excitement and crowds gathered to witness the 'drop'. A market garden now occupies the site.

Tibberton is served by two places of worship. The Primitive Methodist chapel was built in 1842. The present parish church of All Saints was built in 1843 near the site of an old 12th century church. It holds 140 people, has three beautiful memorial stained glass windows and a peal of five bells. A clock in the tower is the village war memorial.

Tibberton Church of England school is thriving in the village. It is a new school, opened in 1970, and children from surrounding villages are bussed in and out each day.

No account about Tibberton would be complete without mentioning Cherrington, a small hamlet 1 mile to the west. Cherrington Manor, an old moated farmhouse dominates the scenery. At its rear stands the old Malt House which started off the world famous nursery rhyme:

'This is the house that Jack built'

Built in 1635 the outside of Cherrington Manor is a perfect example of black and white Tudor craftsmanship but because of a fire 100 years ago the inside has been modernised. Also in Cherrington are 3 cruck houses. This isolated little pocket dating back to the 15th century is unique in that it is the only example of cruck houses in this part of Shropshire. These houses retain many of their original structures.

Ticklerton

Ticklerton in 1987 is a village of private homes, some very old others more modern. Lower Farm and Upper Farm still continue in traditional agriculture but there is no longer a smithy, pub or shop. The village has two impressive houses, Hall Farm and Ticklerton Court.

The village hall was built by public subscription, local people holding dances and whist drives in nearby farms and houses to raise the money. The first Christmas whist drive in 1927 was so well attended that many people had to play at tables set up at the Court. Children's Christmas parties became a feature of village life and continue in exactly the same style to this day. Over the years Coronation and Jubilee celebrations have been organised with teas, sports, tug of war, dances and drama productions. The village took part in a pageant in Ludlow Castle to celebrate the Silver Jubilee of George V.

In the early years of this century Jack Miles used to travel around the farms killing pigs. He also owned a cider press which was hauled by horse and cart to each farm as they needed it. At that time Cox's Barn at Upper Farm was used to hold the local dances. A piano and fiddle provided the music, the fiddler being Elijah Finch, and a carpet was hired to cover the brick floor.

The only new buildings in the village are the 4 council houses which were built in 1952. Today the County Plan does not allow any new development other than for agricultural purposes so the village will remain in its present form for many years to come.

Tilstock ✒

In the autumn of 1967 and the spring of 1968 the scourge of foot and mouth disease struck the village and the surrounding area. Since that time the pattern of farming has changed dramatically. Most farms were dairy and included farmhouse cheesemakers but now several farms in and around the village are arable, growing grain, potatoes, carrots, sugarbeet, beans, and peas, with some beef and winter sheep from the Welsh hills. The big bale silage has replaced the haycocks in the fields and the combine has replaced the binder, the stooks of corn, and the threshing box.

Christ Church Tilstock, built in 1836, celebrated its 150th year in 1986 and was redecorated for the occasion. With a new carpet and the church brasses all bright and shining, together with the spectacular flower arrangements the church looked very beautiful and attracted many visitors from a very wide area.

The Bowling Club began its life on the Vicarage lawn but in 1948 land was purchased and two tennis courts and a bowling green were laid. Thus the Tilstock Tennis and Bowling Club was formed. In 1976 a new Club House was built and floodlighting has since been installed. It now hosts the County Cup matches on the green.

Much housing development has taken place in recent years and the population considerably increased. However sadly, in the name of prog-

Maltkiln Cottages, Tilstock

ress – or planner's folly – beautiful half timbered properties have been demolished.

The Springwood Nursery on the fringe of the village has a large selection of trees, shrubs and heathers and specializes in rhododendrons which attract customers from far afield. The village has a school, a playgroup, two shops, a post office and an inn. Tilstock is altogether a thriving village.

Tong

Three miles to the east of the ancient market town of Shifnal lies the pretty village of Tong, just off the main A41 road. The church, its spire rising from the centre, stands up with striking beauty, dominating the village and well deserves the title of the most beautiful village church in Shropshire – the village Westminster Abbey. It was built in 1410 by Lady

Elizabeth Pembruge in memory of her husband Sir Fulke de Pembruge, but over the centuries has seen many changes and acquired many treasures.

The grave of Dickens' Little Nell is pointed out to visitors. Opposite the church is a row of black and white cottages also associated with Dickens' *Old Curiosity Shop.* Just beyond the cottages stands the old village school which closed 25 years ago.

Well within living memory children wore buttonholes of oak apples on 29th May and sang 'Oak Apple Day, Oak Apple Day, if they don't give us a holiday we will all run away'. The afternoon of 29th May was a half-day holiday, in memory of Charles II who was sheltered by the Pendrells of nearby Boscobel after the Battle of Worcester and who returned to the throne on 29th May, 1660. Any child without an oak apple was chased by school fellows with stinging nettles.

Tong Castle was on the same side of the village roadway as the church, the remains of the main gateway to the castle are still to be seen. The castle, unoccupied since the First World War was destroyed in 1954 after a child fell to his death climbing the walls of the ruined building. The threat of the loss of the site of the castle, by burial forever under the M54, caused an extensive archaeological 'dig'.

Many changes have taken place in the life of the village this century, not only has the school closed but also the post office, village shop, tailors, boot repairers, wheelwright, blacksmith, undertakers, in fact every attribute that made village life. Tong as a village name has had many spellings over past centuries, in Domesday it was Tuange. According to an eminent Shropshire archaeologist the most likely derivation is from Thong – Thong-lands, lands of Thanes or Barons.

Uffington 🐚

The village of Uffington is situated 3 miles north of Shrewsbury. It is bounded to the south by the river Severn, and nestles in the lee of Haughmond Hill, which not only provides a pleasant backdrop, but some protection from the northerly winds.

A mixture of old (some black and white) and newer properties are positioned in close proximity on either side of the road for about half a mile and constitute the main part of the village.

The church of the Holy Trinity is of early English style, restored in 1856 and seats 160 people. The Corbet Arms public house has been, and still is, the local hostelry. The white, double fronted, building has changed little over the years.

Many remember Bill Stevens the ferryman. He pulled his boat by means of a taut wire rope over the river from Monkmoor fields to terminate near his cottage just down behind the church.

The old canal (now filled in, and a public footpath) ran through Uffington to Castlefields and probably was used to transport the coal.

One mile north west of Uffington stood a handsome mansion known as Sundorne Castle built circa 1820 and standing in 80 acres of parkland. This was the home of the Corbet family who owned the Sundorne estate. It was demolished in 1956 leaving the chapel standing. This building, today, is in reasonable condition with lovely stained glass windows, timbered roofing and Jackfield tiled floor – quite the most ornate hay barn in Europe!

A little further north are the ruins of the 12th century Haughmond Abbey, well preserved, and in the hands of National Heritage and open to the public.

Haughmond Hill is an elevated rocky plateau and local beauty spot of some 1 to 2 square miles. The Forestry Commission are felling and replanting trees and have opened up many new walking tracks. A reservoir is situated on the edge facing the Wrekin.

It is hoped that Uffington will not lose its identity by becoming engulfed in the urban sprawl which gets closer. Perhaps the penalty one pays for having the best of both worlds.

Upton Cressett

Although less than 3 miles from Bridgnorth, Upton Cressett seems very remote and hardly part of the 20th century. It is unusual too, in that there are two roads to Upton Cressett, serving either end of the parish, but if travellers ask the way they will have to give a specific destination, or they may receive wrong directions which would involve them in a 6 mile return journey, as there is no way through!

The older and more historical part of Upton Cressett is approached by a very steep road climbing through the woods on Meadowley Bank, which followed to its end, through a ford, leads to the Hall, a very beautiful rose-red brick house with a fine Elizabethan gatehouse. It has been a long held tradition that the young Princes spent a night here in

163

1483, on their way from their imprisonment in Ludlow Castle to their subsequent death in the Tower of London.

Close to the Hall stands the now redundant church of St Michael and All Angels. Built on a Saxon site it has a chancel arch of exceptional size for so small a church. It was built as a private chapel and there is a particularly fine Norman font.

An amusing modern legend, frequently regaled, concerns the plight of the wife of a poor farmer in the 1920s. The threshing box, complete with its gang of 10 or 12 men was due to arrive. By tradition the men had to be fed and the where-with-all to do this was not available. The distraught lady had no money, a very common state of affairs in those hard times, and to provide rabbit or fat boiled bacon or even ancient boiled hen would have involved considerable loss of face. Inspiration came to her rescue, and during the night she crept out to dig up the remains of a large stag turkey, killed by a fox the previous week. Unknown to her, the exhumation had been witnessed by the gossipy young girl she employed. Two days later the threshing gang sat expectantly while the turkey with full trimmings was set before them. The gang leader rose to his feet and called for a toast, the threshers all stood raising their mugs. The leader, respectfully removing his cap, gave the toast:- 'Here's to the Missus, and here's to the Boss and here's R.I.P. to the CHURKEY that's bin buried too long!' At which the whole gang filed away from the table. Legend does not record on what, if anything, they subsequently dined!

Upton Magna 🌿

A few miles off the A5, snuggling below the southern side of beautiful Haughmond Hill, lies the thriving village community of Upton Magna. Once part of the vast Sundorne estate, this village has all the ingredients for survival with shop and post office, church, school, pub and blacksmith.

All approach roads are dominated by the view of the impressive perpendicular tower of the church of St Lucia, one of only two churches dedicated to the saint in this country. This lovely old church has its foundations in the 12th century and contains interesting monuments and artifacts that convey some of the past history of the village.

Heavy industry has never gained a foothold in or around the village, although at Upton Forge, one mile out of the village, the links were cast for the Menai Suspension Bridge, built by Thomas Telford, and sent via the canal system to Anglesey. The Shropshire Union Canal, alas now almost filled in and overgrown, skirts the village and was once the scene of great activity, with barges carrying coal and feedstuffs. Almost parallel with the line of the canal runs the Shrewsbury to Wellington railway line, the railways having arrived in 1849.

The land around the village has been intensively farmed over the last few decades, with loss of hedgerows and headlands, but shelter belts and areas of woodland have been planted recently along with hundreds of trees. The land lends itself to field sports, the Beagles meet at the Corbet Arms, twice yearly and the North Shropshire Hunt has visited the village. Game shooting has always been popular here and according to the old game registers of 1836, many partridges were shot, some of which were sent to Dr Darwin of Shrewsbury, one wonders if they were eaten to celebrate the return of his famous son Charles. Today due to changed farming techniques the partridge numbers have drastically declined, reared pheasants now taking their place in the game registers.

Opposite the school playing fields, under a spreading chestnut tree the village smithy stands. Here the blacksmith, or farrier as we have today, has worked as long as any villager can remember. Facing the smithy is the Corbet Arms.

Upton Magna is a forward looking village, lively and active, yet still retains its rural appeal and rustic charm.

Walford & Walford Heath

Walford is a township and small village within Baschurch parish, of which the main estate consisted of Walford Manor, now an agricultural college. The sole landowner was Thomas Slaney-Eyton Esq D.L. J.P. who resided at Walford Hall.

Yeaton-Peavery stood in a park of 250 acres, and part of this was made into a school for girls known as St Margaret's. This was closed about 1970. There was also an infant school at Walford built in 1853 for 40 children which was supported by the Baschurch School Trustees.

Local crafts included a shoemaker and a wheelwright. Mr Arthur Speke was a blacksmith and carpenter at what is now Walford Garage. He used to have about 20 people working there, either as qualified workers or apprentices.

Avon House used to be a public house known as The Buck or Bucks Head, whilst there was an off-licence beerhouse at Walford Heath Farm.

165

The local shop used to be at the present home of Meadowside and there was also a shop at Old Woods, next to the pub which used to be called The Railway Inn.

At one time about 60 years ago there was no train stop at Old Woods and the local people had to walk to Leaton Station to get into Shrewsbury. Some people owned a pony and trap and stables were provided at the Primitive Methodist Chapel for the visiting preacher or any of the congregation to stable their horse. Before the mains water was piped to Walford the residents used to use the village pump which was (and still is) sited on the opposite side of the road to the Chapel.

Waters Upton 🌿

Waters Upton is a small village situated on an ancient site. In the Domesday Book it was called Uptone. It was later known as Upton Parva (meaning small) to distinguish it from other Uptons. In the year 1200 it had a population of 200 and an area of 730 acres, which included one large farm. Walter Fitzjohn, who owned the Manor in 1200, changed the name to Walters Upton. Later in 1272 it finally became Waters Upton.

The river Tern forms the boundary on the north east side of the village, into which the river Meese flows from Great Bolas. At the junction where the two rivers meet, huge stepping stones were placed to enable people to visit Great Bolas and Cold Hatton. This spot was called Nobridge and although a bridge was built over the river later to make a public footpath, the area is still known by its old name.

The first church was built in the 11th century, being a chapelry of High Ercall, but became a separate parish in the 16th century. In 1865 the whole church was demolished and a larger one erected with local sandstone.

Across the road from the church still stands 'the old priest's house' (which has only recently been modernised) where the monks stayed after journeying from Shrewsbury on the Saturday to attend mass the following day, before returning to the Abbey.

In 1703 John Wase, a wealthy haberdasher from Shrewsbury, modernised the Hall considerably to make a suitable Queen Anne frontage. Interesting features of the Hall include a dairy and a cider press in the cellar, with a 40 foot deep stone-dressed circular well and cruckbeam construction. Pack horse steps from the garden suggest that the house is on the route of an old pack horse route. It is pretty certain that the front lawn was once the village green until it was enclosed sometime during the 19th century.

Some of the old names of Waters Upton consisted of the Bennetts and Butters, who were shoemakers. The Ridgways were the blacksmiths for a century. It is said that John Ridgway gave all his savings to build Waters Upton chapel.

Today there are 5 farms in the village, which are mainly arable. Dairy farming has decreased due to the new agricultural regulations. Council houses were built in the 1950s and more recently some private residences, but even so the population still remains at 220. Telford New Town is only a few miles away, let us hope it does not come any nearer!

Wattlesborough 🦢

Wattlesborough lies on the A458 Shrewsbury to Welshpool road near the Welsh border.

Mainly a farming area, the village has a thriving community which centres around the local village hall. The hall itself was once an army building at Prees Heath during the First World War. It was purchased by local people and brought to Wattlesborough in 1920. It is still in daily use by playgroups, local choirs, variety concerts and pantomimes and weekly whist drives and dances.

The village has both a chapel and a church. The Methodist chapel is built of red brick and sandstone, dated 1893. The church is named after St Margaret of Scotland. It is also of brick, being built in 1931. On the opposite side of the road lies the now empty Church of England school. It was built in 1871 of local stone and brick, with brick additions built on since the Second World War. The building boasts unusual 'twisted' style brick chimneys which are also to be found on the neighbouring farmhouse. In the mid 1970s the school was transferred approximately 100 yards up the road to Wigmore Lane where about 60 children of primary age attend.

Nearby stands an ancient monument, Wattlesborough Castle Tower which dates back to the late 12th century. It is 42 feet square and about 50 feet high, with walls 6 feet thick. It originally had three storeys, but is now a mere shell. It is connected to an earthwork and moat which probably formed one of the fortified strongholds which stretched across the district.

Wattlesborough was first mentioned in the Domesday Book as Wetesburg, it is probably derived from the Anglo-Saxon name of Waetels-borough. One theory is that it could have originated from houses built with wattle and daub walls.

Welsh Frankton 🐟

Whichever way you enter the village you have to climb. From Whittington there is Gannon Hill. Before you come over the canal bridge there is the only inn in the area called the Narrow Boat Inn, opened during these last few years. It was once a farmworker's cottage and from here one can hire pleasure boats for trips on the canal. From Ellesmere you come up the Brow, and when you reach the top there is a magnificent panoramic view of the Shropshire hills, the Breiddens, and Berwyns of Wales.

One could say that the village is in 3 parts – the centre, Perthy, and Lower Frankton which has a number of farms and cottages, and also leads you to the Shropshire Union Canal and the Montgomery branch. The centre consists of a few houses, a filling station and garage and a post office which until recently was also the village shop. The lovely church of St Andrew built in the 1850s has beautiful stained glass windows and is well preserved, only marred perhaps by the number of stone steps in order to gain access.

For the last two years or so Welsh Frankton has started a scheme which is highly successful called 'Country Village Week-end Breaks', when for six week-ends between April and October the village plays host to small groups of visitors. Local homes cater for bed and breakfast, and village organisations such as the Women's Institute and individuals entertain them from Friday evening through to Sunday lunch. This venture has proved a great success, villagers and visitors mix well and it has also brought young and old closer together.

In September 1987 four restored locks were opened on the Montgomeryshire branch of the Shropshire Union Canal. These locks form a vital part of long-term work to restore the 35 mile long Montgomery Canal, which was built between 1793 and 1821 connecting the national network with Welshpool and Newtown. Abandoned in 1936 it is now being restored with work undertaken by the British Waterway Board and volunteers from all over the country. A walk along the towpath shows locks and aqueducts, wharfs and lime kilns from the canal's working past. There is a colourful variety of plants and wild life, including kingfishers, herons, swans and wild ducks.

Wentnor 🌿

Wentnor is a village of 24 dwellings set on a ridge 900 feet above sea level, half-way between the Long Mynd and the Stiperstones.

It has a church, restored in 1886 at a cost of £1,200, which has a Norman doorway and window of at least 900 years old. The entrance is 13th century, the reredos is mosaic work in an alabaster frame and the pulpit is carved oak of the period of James I.

In the baptistry is the famous hurricane tombstone, which is a memorial to a family who lived at the foot of the Long Mynd and who perished when their house was buried under an avalanche many years ago.

There is a public house where, in the early part of the century the Morris family were Maltsters. The village now has a post office stores and to the west a modern campsite with its own inn.

Life has changed enormously over the last 30 years when most people earned their living from farming. Nowadays, most people commute to neighbouring towns.

On the edge of Wentnor, off the Adstone Lane, is a field called the Black Graves and Groaning Stile where it is reputed people were buried during the Black Death.

The inhabitants of Wentnor, together with local villages, still have the right to cut peat on the Long Mynd.

Westbury 🌿

Westbury, as its name implies, is on the road out of Shrewsbury to the west, and this has always been vastly important to the village. Mentioned in the Domesday Book as Westburie, the village was already important as it had a collegiate church with two rectors. A castle was then built on a knoll just west of the village by Roger Fitz Corbet, who had fought at Hastings. A motte and bailey castle, it was named Caus after Corbet's birthplace in Normandy. It stood for centuries until burnt down during the Civil War, but its stone foundations are there for all to see.

A dreadful murder took place in Westbury in 1907 resulting in a hanging in Shrewsbury Gaol, and the legend of a ghostly bloodstained mark of a hand that could not be erased, on the wall of the inn.

Richard Wigley, a butcher of Shrewsbury cut the throat of Mary Eliza Bowen, a barmaid at The Lion Hostelry on the main road west out of the village. He 'did it for love', but it was a very gory murder and the poor dying girl staggered into the passage of the inn from the back stairs, placing a blood-stained hand on the wall before expiring. Washed many times with soapy water and covered with limewash, the ghostly hand-mark could not be erased, until finally the old hostelry was demolished in 1965 to make way for a modern Lion Hotel.

Westbury's future is promising. This is mainly due to the mundane fact of having sewerage laid on in 1985. Before that the nuisance of septic tanks kept the village small, and hindered development, but now the village is in the 20th century with a vengeance and many new houses are being built. This means more children at the village school and both school and post office are no longer in danger of the axe. Not more than 300 people live in the village proper, but the surrounding farms and hamlets provide another 2,000 souls.

On Mayday Westbury has a Spring Festival that has its parallel in the Westbury Wakes held in the churchyard at Candlemas. This fair finished in 1282 but its components have a familiar ring, for plays, mummers, stalls, ales and games are just what happens on Mayday today and the venue is not more than 100 yards from the site of the fair of the 13th century.

West Felton 🦢

West Felton, an Anglo Saxon village, is situated in the north west of the county. 'Fel' means fall of the tree and 'ton' means landed gentry or squires. The 'West' was added, probably around the 12th century, when the drapers would rest on the way from Shrewsbury to the very important woollen market in Oswestry. The wool packer's stone can still be seen by the Punch Bowl Inn.

Life has changed over the years. Farming, with meadows called Fairyland, Lords Cross, Rising Sun, was the main work in the area, so the houses were built in hamlets around the farms and estates. The area boasted 9 blacksmiths in earlier times – an important asset to the village life. Between 1844 and 1862 the village had a curfew bell that rang everyday at 5 am and 7 pm. The farm workers relied on this bell for getting to work on time and all the children had to be in the house by the 7 pm bell. A fayre was held once a year during the 1800s for one day. Usually the whole village turned out unless sick or infirm. Sports, roundabouts and swings, plenty to watch or take part in. At twilight it finished with a tug-of-war and dancing until midnight.

The area had a glass factory and during the war there was the RAF base. Today there is the post office, the school, 2 public houses and a Military Museum. Many of the farms have disappeared. Most people travel out of West Felton for their work. Life was difficult with the A5 running through the village but now there is the bypass taking the heavy traffic away and bringing in developments of large expensive houses. Fortunately there is still a village atmosphere and there are activities for young and old.

Among the interesting buildings there is the 11th century church of St Michael, situated in the west of the village. Behind the church stood a castle, moat and bridge.

St Winifred's Well, Woolston, sprang up where her body rested on its way from Holywell to Shrewsbury. A black and white building stands over the spring, said to have healing powers for the eyes. Bishop's Well is where the Bishop washed his feet after resting on the Bishop's stone, now on Bishop's Corner. Threadneedle Well was the first source of water, in the 11th century, for Felton.

Weston Lullingfields 🌿

Weston Lullingfields, lying 11 miles northwest of Shrewsbury, and 2 miles north of Baschurch, consists of 3 hamlets (Weston Lullingfields, Weston Common and Weston Wharf) with outlying farms and houses.

Weston Lullingfields has always been an agricultural community with, in the 19th and early 20th centuries, at least 25 farmers, some of them called 'cowkeepers' or 'cottage farmers'. Farming in the area is traditionally dairy.

A few cottages lacked electricity and inside water until recently, but most have been modernised. The latter, and new houses and bungalows built in the last 20 or so years, are often inhabited by people from outside the area. The County Council provided a few smallholdings between the wars and some council houses were built.

Weston Lullingfields was in the ecclesiastical parish of Baschurch until a separate parish was formed and a church and vicarage built in 1857. Now the two parishes are again under the care of one vicar and the vicarage is a private house.

An important event in the history of the village occurred when a branch of the Ellesmere canal reached Weston and there stopped for lack of money in 1797. Weston Wharf became a busy place, with its warehouse, limekilns, stables, weighing machine, clerk's house and the Boat Inn. Cottages were built near the wharf and along the road from Weston Common. Large quantities of lime, slate, coal and other goods were brought in by barge and collected by horses and carts from the surrounding area, while timber, cheese and farm products were loaded into the returning barges. The chains for the Menai Bridge were brought from Shrewsbury by road to be shipped from the Wharf in 1825. All this activity was declining before 1914 and, when the bank burst in 1934, it was left unrepaired until finally the canal was filled in.

Within living memory a tailor used to sit working cross-legged in his cottage and a woman and her two daughters ran a laundry at Dumpling Hall – named from the round tied-up bundles of washing. A post office was opened at one of the general stores before the First World War; both shop and post office were closed in the 1970s. The other shop, at Weston Common, closed in 1941. The last butcher's shop, with fields for grazing and outhouses for slaughtering lasted until 1976.

The modern village still has a sense of communtiy – for instance, money was raised in the 1960s to build a village hall, which was opened in 1968 and enlarged in 1978, and there is a voluntary car scheme. Surrounded by green fields and with wonderful views towards the Welsh mountains and the Shropshire hills, the village is a pleasant place.

Weston Rhyn 🍂

The village of Weston Rhyn is a scattered collection of small hamlets on the Clwyd border about 4 miles from the market town of Oswestry. If you stand with your back to St John's Anglican church you will be in the centre of the village and at the meeting of the five-ways. One of these will take you past the Village Institute and up through Quinta and Bronygarth to the old turnpike road which leads to the north west border of the village, the river Ceiriog and Offa's Dyke path. Nearby are the lime kilns which produced the first slaked lime for agricultural use, distributed throughout the area by the Shropshire Union canal.

If you decide to follow the old High Street you will pass the ornate Victorian Sunday School building with its turrets and unique ceramic patterned walls built by a local benefactor Thomas Barnes, MP for Bolton.

From another lane you can see Tyn y Rhos Hall which has recently been described as a fine example of a gentleman's minor border country seat in the Tudor style. Earlier, in 1165 during the reign of Henry II, the Prince of Wales, Owain Gwynedd, slept in the house. It is open during summer months to visitors.

Throughout the parish of Weston Rhyn are small, solid stone houses built between 200 and 300 years ago. One of the oldest is situated in the hamlet of Bronygarth overlooking the beautiful Ceiriog Valley. It had two small rooms downstairs and one large loft upstairs reached by a ladder for sleeping. It was once the home of the village cobbler who collected and delivered boots and shoes in his small trap.

Visitors today will no longer find the old industries producing coal and pig iron, or the paper mills which produced paper for the early 'Bradshaws'. The men of Weston Rhyn no longer work down the mines and the nearby Ifton colliery closed many years ago. The only child labour used is for newspaper deliveries and the cornflour mills are residential homes, 'Big Nancy' cannot now be seen carrying coal on her head from the small local pit in Preesgweene, and many a modern busy housewife is glad that she no longer has to haul her washing up to the communal mangle at Tyn y Rhos Lodge. She and her family also value the bakers with its home-made bread and cakes, the post office and stores, the paper shop and butchers, the hairdressers and fish and chip shop. All six pubs have their own snooker, darts and domino teams. There is a fine football team and the mixed choir gives concerts regularly.

Weston-under-Redcastle 🌿

Weston-under-Redcastle is situated about ½ mile off the A49, about half way between Whitchurch and Shrewsbury. It is a very picturesque village with a variety of architecture, ranging from black and white to modern houses, and has a hotel (Hawkstone Park Hotel) with two 18-hole golf courses, where the 1986 British Open Champion, Sandy Lyle, learnt to play golf and until recently lived in the village.

In Saxon times Weston was known as Westune. In 1227 Henry III gave the then owner of the Manor permission to build the Castle of Radecliff and from that time the Manor was known as Weston-under-Redcastle.

Hawkstone Hall and Park was owned by the Hill family from 1554 and the Red Castle was purchased by the family in the early 18th century.

The castle was already a ruin and can still be seen today. Hawkstone Hall is now a Roman Catholic Seminary.

Hawkstone Park and Hawk Lake (which was man-made – partly by prisoners of war from the Peninsular War) were once in the grounds belonging to Hawkstone Hall and include caves, known as The Grotto. The Obelisk is a landmark which can be seen for many miles around – this had a statue on top of Sir Roland Hill but sadly the statue fell into disrepair some years ago. Hawkstone Park was used as a camp for German prisoners of war during the Second World War.

The present church in the village, known as the Chapel of St Luke, was built in 1791, chiefly paid for by Sir Richard Hill, although registers date back to 1565. There are stocks situated on the road-side, by the church, but it is not known how long they have been there or when they were last used!

Wheathill 🌿

Wheathill is not vastly different today to what it was in Norman times. The Manor then consisted of 4 hamlets, Wheathill, Bromdon, Egerton and Leverdegreene (Cold Green), the last two now gone, but the sites known. The fields were all open, commonly grazed and cultivated. Over the ages the fields were gradually enclosed but there are still signs of ancient ridge and furrow cultivation. Common grazing finally ended in 1810 when Cold Green was enclosed and fields granted in exchange for common rights.

The 'Brethren' came to Bromdon in 1942, a community group that originated in Germany. They lived and worked together, farming, fencing, forestry and they had their own school, they finally left in 1963.

Wheathill has a small Norman church, a public house and Youth Hostel.

Loughton is a joint parish with a small 17th century church, on an older site in which stands a yew tree that is one of the oldest living trees in Shropshire, carbon dated to be more than 1,000 years old. Loughton school was the centre of education for Wheathill, Loughton, Aston Botterell and Burwarton, until a school was built in Burwarton in 1864, closing in 1947.

Whittington 🌿

Whittington is a fascinating mixture of buildings, dating from the medieval to the modern. The oldest building, Whittington Castle, stands grey-stoned and massive, reflected in its moat which reaches the roadside. Following the Civil War, the castle fell into disuse, and stone was taken from its walls to repair roads. However, the gatehouse survives intact, its twin towers each side of 6 inch thick studded door, which leads into the castle grounds and the outer bailey. Here, circular steps lead to the top of the ruins, where children delight to climb while adults admire the view.

Three centres of worship still stand to serve the community – a Methodist chapel at Babbinswood, a United Reform church and the church of St John the Baptist, which is sited opposite the castle. There was once a medieval chapel on the site, with a register dating back to 1591, but the present Italianate style church was built in 1749.

In the centre of the village is a row of Tudor-style bungalows designed for senior citizens and completed in 1986. Opposite the bungalows is the newly cleared Donnet Corner, a pleasant tree-filled triangle, behind which is the black and white 18th century Old Post House.

The Park Hall estate was once the grounds of a gracious 16th century hall, which burned down in 1917, when Park Hall was a camp for 60,000 troops. Remembered by many Second World War soldiers, the camp buildings have been cleared and much of the land returned to agricultural and residential use. It is now the venue for Oswestry Agricultural Show, and provides facilities for rugby, shooting, hockey, football and cricket and has an Athletics Stadium. There is also a concealed gypsy encampment, as well as woods used by schools for environmental studies.

Whitton 🌿

Whitton gets its name from the Lords of Whitton. The earliest mentioned is William de Whitton who attested a Charter of Osborn Fitz Hugh in 1174. The estate passed through various hands until it was finally split up in 1920.

Whitton Court is a charming Elizabethan mansion with an old black and white wing facing a courtyard at the rear. On the walls of the dining

175

room are a selection of 14th century murals and the one over the fireplace is purported to be the Whitton family taking part in a stag hunt.

St Mary's church at Whitton is part Norman, with some Victorian addition.

The Hollins is a genuine old black and white property lying about ½ mile from Whitton Court and believed at one time to have been the Dower House to the Court.

Canal Cottage Whixall: a typical Thomas Telford design

Whitton had a school but this closed in 1952 and is now a private residence. Many of the people who attended the school as children still live locally.

Unfortunately for the peace of Whitton the 20th century has caught up. At one end of the village is a large poultry farm and at the Greete end a large turkey unit has appeared.

Whixall

Whixall is situated in the extreme north west corner of Shropshire and is somewhat unique in that there is no actual village. Instead it is a scattered spread of properties covering the whole area. Visitors are usually unaware they have arrived in Whixall until they see the signs directing them back the way they have just come!

Agriculture has been and still is the main industry of the area, as the soil is dark and fertile. A large proportion of the fields are relatively small ranging from 2 to 12 acres, ideal for the many market gardeners who used to work them. In the past decade there has been a noticeable decline in this particular section of the industry and these smallholdings are being returned to grass.

One of the last remaining shops in the parish is the Old Smithy, once bustling with horses, now a store selling agricultural goods, brushes, barrows and such items. It still has the blacksmith's forge intact as when it was last used.

Whixall certainly isn't short of places of worship, as there are 5 churches in the parish. They are the Church of England, Congregational, Primitive Methodist, United Reformed, & Wesleyan Methodist.

The Llangollen canal runs through the western side of the parish and is now a very busy waterway, catering for the many holidaymakers who enjoy cruising on it. Work on the section from Ellesmere to Whitchurch started in 1797, and eventually reached Tilstock Park in 1806. Commercial use of the canal ceased in 1936 and some sections went into disuse, then in the 1950s and 1960s came the new lease of life to canals with the arrival of the 'boat' people.

The unique area of Whixall moss is a botanists dream. The vast expanse of peat and bog supports a fascinating range of flora and fauna. Many people rented land in years gone by to cut peat by hand, a backbreaking job, to sell as fuel or grind for compost. Today there are machines to do the job and a busy compost 'factory' supplies many garden centres over a wide area.

Willey 🐛

Willey is mentioned in the Domesday Book. The name was spelt many different ways, Wilileia, Willileg, Williley, and Willey; it means 'the clearing in the willows'.

In 1618 the estate was sold to a Town Clerk of London, John Weld, knighted by Charles I. In 1748 the estate passed by marriage to the Forester family. Their former home, a Tudor house, still stands and is now known as the Old Hall. Their home today is Willey Park which was built by Lewis Watt for the first Lord Forester in 1816.

It is difficult to imagine that here in so quiet a part of Shropshire industry flourished. Willey New Furnace, a place of fields today on the

Broseley/Barrow road was an important part of the Industrial Revolution. Here one of the earliest Boulton and Watt steam engines was set up under the control of James Watt. Also here, using a new boring process, John Wilkinson established himself as a leading ironmaster. The world's first iron boat was built and launched at Willey Wharf on the Severn.

In the past the inhabitants of the village nearly all worked on the estate. Other trades were blacksmiths, millers and furnacemen at the New Willey furnace. Today we find accountants, cabinet makers, restorers of porcelain. People work for the Ironbridge Gorge Museum and each brings his or her own ideas to the life of the village.

Each year in the summer a fun-day is held in the village to raise money for the village hall. This is used by the people of Willey and surrounding district. The village hall was built in 1948. Willey has a thriving cricket club and football club.

Wistanstow

The jewel in Wistanstow's crown has to be the village hall, a magnificent black and white half timbered building with a mock Tudor frontage overlooking the village, with two semi-detached homes, one designated for the District Nurse, the other for the resident caretaker. Beautiful, unique, fully furnished with every item of recreational facility imaginable, even two tennis courts in the grounds. As though that was not enough this entire property was an outright gift to the parish in 1925 from Mrs Harriet Greene of The Grove, dedicated to her late husband's memory.

The Greenes owned the Grove estate, they lived in the country mansion known simply as the Grove (now obsolete) and employed an enormous staff. Their estate took in several thousand acres in this fertile part of South Shropshire, and Wistanstow was the only village on the estate. Though there was a cluster of houses in other places forming hamlets here and there, they all came under the Wistanstow parish.

After the opening ceremony, which some people remember to this day as a wonderful event, the village came alive. Clubs were formed. One very popular addition to the village was the Brass Band.

Mrs Greene's care for her tenants did not end with her death, for she left in her will instructions that every tenant was to have the opportunity to buy the home they lived in as sitting tenants. Most families were able to take up this offer.

Wistanswick 🌿

A hamlet set in acres of green fields, within the parish of Stoke-on-Tern and bordered by the A4 trunk road.

In the past it was mainly on agriculture that the jobs of the locals depended – ploughing, sowing and reaping, in that order, with the horse-drawn implements which now, of course, have been replaced with tractors and combine harvesters. With their coming, jobs dwindled away and the young men were forced to look for jobs in the towns and factories. The only source of employment was the builders yard owned by the Millington family. This yard also employed carpenters and wheelwrights and ran an undertakers business. These jobs too had gone by the 1970s.

The villagers worshipped at the Congregational Church which was the centre of any social life. Many services and meetings were held there including (perhaps not always popular) Temperance meetings. Now the church is called the United Reformed Church after its amalgamation with the Presbyterians.

The villagers must have been and still are very well behaved for no breath of real scandal has filtered through the years. It has had its share of characters like the man nicknamed 'Smokey Jack' who, amongst his many duties, carried the lavatory pans (from the two-seater toilet at the Manse) on the handlebars of his bicycle to be emptied at a discreet distance from all habitation. Other houses, not so lucky, dug a hole in the garden. Wistanswick has always been famed for its good rhubarb.

There are several interesting properties in the village, two black and white and previously thatched, one is still known as the Thatch having the date 1645 carved on the door lintel. The other, Yew Tree Cottage, is reputed to be older still. The Red Lion, the only public house in the village, dates back to the 1700s and has been hosted by the same family for four generations.

Withington 🌿

Withington lies in a low, wide valley with many homes having lovely views to the Stretton Hills, The Wrekin and Haughmond Hill. The Saxon name, Weintone suggests an early settlement among the willows and is mentioned in the Domesday Book.

After 1918 400 acres of The Manor were sold and became 8 Council farms for the war's ex-servicemen. Six distinctive white farmhouses were built about the village and the Manor House and its original buildings became the other two farms. The handsome red brick house bears the inscription 'Illedge and Mary Maddox 1710'.

A church was recorded in 1150 but the pleasant red sandstone building, with its broach spire was newly consecrated in May 1874. Parts of the old church were incorporated in the new.

There are many interesting timbered buildings in the village. These timbered buildings and Church Farm were there when the Shrewsbury Canal was opened in 1797, together with a blacksmith's shop and public house. The canal was dug to carry coal from the Ketley area to Shrewsbury and near the Old Post Office there was a wharf receiving 30 tons of coal a month. The canal was abandoned in 1944 and two lift bridges removed. A few lengths of the canal bed remain in fields. It was a tub-coat canal with tow-path and engineered by Josiah Clowes and Thomas Telford, and passed beside the churchyard wall.

During the last 20 years bungalows and houses have been added in Carnarvon Lane and houses built in Sunnyfields. Others have been extended. The post office closed, but The Hare and Hounds Inn survives. There for many years a Harvest Auction has been held with the proceeds shared between the church and other good causes.

Woolstaston 🐑

This interesting little village is situated on the lower slopes of the Long Mynd hills at 750 feet above sea level. The farms and cottages in the village all have a wealth of oak beams and there has been very little new building for the past hundred or so years.

Snow falls have always been the dread of the community and it was nothing for Woolstaston to be cut off for weeks on end. Thankfully, today things are better with snowploughs, etc. but it can still be three or four days. One of the most memorable stories was when the Rev Carr from Woolstaston Rectory was lost in the snow after taking the service at Ratlinghope. He started to return home on foot and was hopelessly lost and ended up at the Church Stretton end of the Long Mynd. He wrote a book called *A Night in the Snow* which describes how he kept himself awake and was alive to tell the tale. This was in 1865 and the book has recently been reprinted and is well worth reading.

181

Life has changed in this type of village. There is only one farm and the other houses are occupied by professional men and women who work mainly in Telford and Wolverhampton and Shrewsbury. The land has been sold off – mostly bought by neighbouring farmers to increase the size of their farms.

The Walk Mills was a fulling mill and a corn mill, but it is now a very necessary yard for the repair of metalwork or welding.

Woore 🐚

Woore is situated at the junction of the A51 and the A525 so the traffic, which speeds through to North Wales or to nearby Bridgemere Garden World, is considerable. The village is well signposted as there was once a National Hunt race-course here. Enthusiasts of the Dick Francis novels may be interested to learn that he rode his first race at Woore. The three public houses do a brisk trade and on a summer's evening the village is thronged with happy revellers. It is traditional for the Swan Hotel to host the meet of the North Staffordshire Hunt on Boxing Day at which there are many hundreds of spectators every year.

Long before the days of the stage coach Oure, Owre or Woore was an established settlement and mentioned in the Domesday Book. The name meant a border and the village is still on the borders of Shropshire, Staffordshire and Cheshire. Those who indulged in cock-fighting found the situation remarkably convenient as they slipped from county to county, thereby escaping the wrath of the constables who had jurisdiction over one county only.

Woore seems to have always had an ash tree and from time to time a fresh sapling is planted with great ceremony so that the tradition may be continued. At present there is one on the high ground of the old shooting butts and this may have acted as a marker for those travelling across country in a bygone age.

From about 1552 Woore had a chapel-of-ease but in 1830 the land used for the Swan Hotel's stabling was bought for the building of a church. Later a tower was added and the church, painted white in recent years, now has an Italianate appearance. The church is dedicated to St Leonard, patron saint of prisoners, but there is no record of why this unlikely dedication was chosen.

Within the last 15 years a substantial number of new houses has been built behind the church and these have been mainly occupied by commuters. Newcomers mix happily with the older residents and many have used their talents unstintingly for the benefit of the community. From the newcomers the idea of a village concert originated and this is now an annual event. Every January versatile performers put on a lively and almost professional show as a result of which many thousands of pounds have been given to charity.

Worfield 🐾

The picturesque village of Worfield lies on the river Worfe approximately 4 miles north east of Bridgnorth. It is set in one of the largest parishes in England, comprising 30 hamlets scattered over an area of some 20 square miles. All of these are mentioned in the Domesday Book, and have retained their identity up to the present time.

The church of St Peter is the dominating feature of the village. It is built in sandstone, and has the distinction of possessing a lofty spire, which, with the tower below and the vane above, rises 200 feet above the floor of the porch. The church is famous for its annual flower festival, which has taken place for many years, and attracts visitors from far and wide. Another well-known event is the passion play. This has been performed in the church since 1973 at 5-yearly intervals, and was specially written for the parish by the late Michael Lloyd, a local industrialist (choir-master and organist) who unfortunately was tragically killed in a fire before the first production took place.

Years ago, the main occupations would have been milling (grain, paper and cloth) and yeomanry. Farming has been retained today, as the main industry, but due to the innovation of new farming methods, fewer jobs are available on the land and many people have to commute to out-lying industrial areas to find employment.

The majority of the property in the village still belongs to the Davenport estate, and tenants present themselves twice yearly to the Davenport Arms to pay their rent. This popular public house, known locally as The Dog because of the Davenport crest, together with the church, form the hub of the village. The pub itself dates back a bit, and some former tenants were convinced the place was haunted, because their dog would not enter a certain room at any time, and would walk around with hackles raised.

Worthen 🦌

Worthen Brook rises in the hills beyond Rowley and originally three corn mills were driven by its water power – Walton, Brockton and Worthen. Worthen mill varied its functions over the centuries between corn, timber, wool and cider. It was demolished in 1973 to make way for the Millstream estate of 4 houses and 18 bungalows.

However, for many centuries the brook was Worthen's 'power station' and its products were financed and supported by local farmers and other business enterprises. Indeed, Worthen has never lacked industrial and commercial initiative, each generation responding to the demands of its own age. Thus, blacksmiths (4), a ropeworks, stonemason, wheelwright, undertaker, tailor and bakery are now superseded by a garage (with mini supermarket attached), post office and village store, together with a number of builders and decorators, an electrician and a hairdresser. Times change too in other ways, for where once there were 6 pubs, now there are none! Nonetheless, there is no need to go any distance at all to find good company and entertainment. Clubs and societies abound to suit all tastes and ages, most of them centred on the village hall.

Worthen's ancient parish church, founded in Anglo-Saxon times, has a Norman tower, with a ring of 6 bells. The nave is probably of 13th century construction, and a number of interesting additions (together with careful maintenance) bear witness to the goodwill and generosity of many generations of parishioners over the past 800 years.

Proof that 'higher authority' has faith in Worthen's future must surely lie in the fact that the Primary School was moved to a brand new building in 1986, transferred from its original site, where the school had been since its foundation in 1874.

Wrockwardine 🦌

The village of Wrockwardine lies 9 miles east of Shrewsbury, 2 miles west of Wellington, and 2 miles north of The Wrekin, the famous hill which gives its name to the district around it. The Wrekin, in fact, also gave the name Wrockwardine to the village, since the word seems to be derived from two Cambro-British words, 'worthing' meaning a village, and 'Wrch' meaning that which is high or round. Wrockwardine there-fore means 'the village under the hill (The Wrekin)'. The village is 360 feet above sea level, and its church, the church of St Peter, is a prominent landmark, easily seen from the railway-line which runs across the plain between Shrewsbury and Wellington. Indeed, the church is now a landmark by night as well as by day, being floodlit during the hours of darkness, and easily visible for many miles.

The *parish* of Wrockwardine, as opposed to the *village* of Wrockwardine has for centuries included Admaston, Allscot (now mainly known for the British Sugar factory there which processes all the sugar-beet grown for miles around), Bratton, Burcot, Charlton, Cluddeley, Leaton and Long Lane. Post-war housing development in Admaston and even more recent development at Shawbirch has meant that the parish has grown enormously in population. It is worth noting that Wrockwardine Wood, 4 miles away from Wrockwardine village, was for hundreds of years a detached part of Wrockwardine parish. In 1834 Wrockwardine Wood became a separate parish, but the name still causes strangers to the district much confusion.

The parish of Wrockwardine contains only one building (the church of St Peter) listed as a Grade 1 building, but it contains no less than 50 buildings in Grade 2 ('buildings of special interest which warrant every effort being made to preserve them'). These include Orleton Hall, Wrockwardine Hall and the Old Vicarage in the village itself.

The village has a Church of England Primary School, a church hall which serves the church and the village well, and one shop (including post office), as well as several thriving societies.

Yockleton ✤

Much has changed since the days of the Domesday Book, but now as then Yockleton and its surrounding hamlets is a thriving agricultural community. Milk production forms the greater part of the farming activity, with cereals, pig and poultry rearing all being well established. In fact cereals are traditional in the village as the Bromley family at The Lynches, Nox, were maltsters to the area back in the late 18th century, and founded The Maltings in Shrewsbury.

Closely allied to the farming community was the village blacksmith, and there has been a forge at Nox since the middle of the 17th century when two brothers, Richard and John Knox, set up business. The present traditional blacksmith, Mr Eddie Price, has been there for 60 years. Before that his mother ran the business together with a shop, which

The Forge, Yockleton

closed in 1951. In what is now the garden of the forge there was a wheelwright who also doubled up as a coffin maker. Close by there was a cobbler who ran a personal collection and delivery service, and who did all his repairs by candlelight, even when electricity was available.

The church of the Holy Trinity was consecrated in 1861. The village school – a Church school – and the vicarage were also completed at much the same time. The woodwork and carving in Holy Trinity church were crafted by a carpenter called John Evans. This gentleman is credited with building the first wooden bicycle – a velocipede.

Although the village dates back to Domesday times there are comparatively few really old buildings in the area. The most important, and well documented one is the 15th century Manor Farm at Stoney Stretton.

The most exciting new business is Butterfly World, again at Nox, inaugurated by Mr & Mrs S. Bromley four years ago. This attracts visitors from all over the country to its tropical and temperate butterfly houses, its shop, cafe and the new farm trail.

The new housing development at Brookside Gardens together with the longer established houses and farms, will ensure that the village maintains its mix of people vital to the continuing existence of the community.

Heighton Mill, Chirbury, as it looked in 1928

Index

189